Swamp to the Keys

Florida A&M University, Tallahassee
Florida Atlantic University, Boca Raton
Florida Gulf Coast University, Ft. Myers
Florida International University, Miami
Florida State University, Tallahassee
University of Central Florida, Orlando
University of Florida, Gainesville
University of North Florida, Jacksonville
University of South Florida, Tampa
University of West Florida, Pensacola

Other Books by Johnny Molloy

Trial by Trail: Backpacking in the Smoky Mountains

Day and Overnight Hikes in the Great Smoky Mountains National Park

Best in Tent Camping: Smoky Mountains

Best in Tent Camping: Florida

Day and Overnight Hikes in Shenandoah National Park

Beach and Coastal Camping in Florida

Best in Tent Camping: Colorado

A Paddler's Guide to Everglades National Park

Day and Overnight Hikes in West Virginia's Monongahela National Forest

Best in Tent Camping: West Virginia

The Hiking Trails of Florida's National Forests, Parks, and Preserves

Mount Rogers Outdoor Recreation Handbook

Best in Tent Camping: Tennessee & Kentucky

Long Trails of the Southeast

Land Between the Lakes Outdoor Recreation Guide

60 Hikes within 60 Miles: Nashville

Best in Tent Camping: Wisconsin

Best in Tent Camping: Carolinas

Visit the author's web site: www.johnnymolloy.com

Johnny Molloy

University Press of Florida

Gainesville Tallahassee Tampa Boca Raton Pensacola Orlando Miami Jacksonville Ft. Myers

FROM THE

Swamp

TO THE Keys

A Paddle through Florida History

HUDSON BRANCH

08 07 06 05 04 03   6 5 4 3 2 1

Library of Congress Cataloging-in-Publication Data
Molloy, Johnny, 1961–
From the swamp to the Keys: a paddle through Florida history / Molloy, Johnny.
p. cm.
ISBN 0-8130-2622-9 (acid-free paper)
1. Florida—Description and travel. 2. Florida—History, Local.
3. Suwannee River (Ga. and Fla.)—Description and travel. 4. Gulf Coast (Fla.)—
Description and travel. 5. Molloy, Johnny, 1961 —Journeys—Florida. 6. Canoes
and canoeing—Florida. I. Title.
F316.2 .M65 2003
917.59'80464—dc21   2002040903

Front cover photo by Aaron Marabel.
Frontispiece and back cover photos by Charles Dees.

The University Press of Florida is the scholarly publishing agency for the State
University System of Florida, comprising Florida A&M University, Florida Atlantic
University, Florida Gulf Coast University, Florida International University, Florida
State University, University of Central Florida, University of Florida, University of
North Florida, University of South Florida, and University of West Florida.

University Press of Florida
15 Northwest 15th Street
Gainesville, FL 32611-2079
http://www.upf.com

This book is for my adventurous sister-in-law, Tinian.

Contents

Part 1

THE River

Why Do It?

Georgia Highway 177. Two lanes of decaying blacktop. On either side grew pine woods. Chris and I traveled east, to the headwaters of the Suwannee River, or so we hoped. I was uncertain exactly where to begin, even after looking at maps and making a few phone calls. Some distance ahead were the gates of the Okefenokee National Wildlife Refuge. We had planned to begin the trip there, but it was closed to overnight paddlers because of low water. South Georgia and northeastern Florida were in the midst of a drought. We couldn't start in the Okefenokee.

The tall roadside pines flashed steadily by until they seemed like the repetitive background of 1960s cartoon. I finally spotted a rusting, faded metal sign by a mailbox, the first indication of civilization for miles. *Griffis Camp*. I turned, hoping the place was still operating. On the left, beneath a wide-spreading live oak, was an old wooden house, painted green, with a roof so covered in leaves that I didn't know if it could shed water or not. A pay phone attached to a nearby shed looked oddly out of place. A small sign declared: "$2.00 launch fee, Put money in mailbox." The peeling white receptacle had a small hole cut into it for dropping in the money.

We got out of the car, unsurprised by the early January chill that had held Dixie in its grasp for more than a week, sending subfreezing temperatures as far south as Orlando. Chris inspected the grounds while I pushed a doorbell attached to the decaying abode. I doubted an answer, and indeed no one came to the door. Instead, a smiling man came around the side of the house. "Johnny Molloy," I said, sticking out my hand, wondering how such a well-dressed man could emerge from behind such a decrepit shack.

"Al Griffis," he replied. We shook hands as I inquired about launching my canoe and leaving my Jeep for a while. He was evidently pleased to have a visitor and came around to answering my questions, after telling us he was a taxidermist. He offered to show us some of his current works. Being in an adventurous mood, we obliged. We followed the white-haired gentleman, obviously content in his own skin, as he strode across the road onto a short grassy path to a much more habitable house overlooking a crystal clear pond. There was a shed behind it. Into the shed we followed Al. "Here are some deer mounts I'm working on," he said. On the floor were two fresh deer heads. We nodded approvingly, then I once again inquired about the launch fee, realizing I was ready to get on the water. This adventure had been in the works for some time. Al led us into the cabin beside the shed. Once inside, he showed us more of his works: on the wall were three largemouth bass he had caught in the Okefenokee Swamp.

We hesitantly followed Al as he led us into the bedroom where his brother Lem, the owner of the launch place, was lying in bed half covered by a blanket and wearing a heavy coat. Lem had fallen off a ladder while repairing a roof, breaking some ribs. Al pointed to the mount of a large bear on the wall. And it *was* a large bear—three hundred pounds fully dressed out, he told us. Lem an-

The dark waters of the Suwannee, a mere twenty feet wide at this point, contrasted against a white sand shoreline. Chris posed for a picture. Then it was time to head south.

nounced the price for launching the canoe and leaving my car behind: ten dollars. He pulled out change for a twenty from his wallet beside the bed. We felt for the poor man, trapped in the bed. He looked bored out of his mind. Arrangements made, Chris and I drove the Jeep to the riverside launch, just a sandy break in the wooded swamp surrounding the Suwannee River.

The afternoon sun fell in frail beams across the river. The dark waters of the not-so-broad Suwannee, a mere twenty feet wide at this point, contrasted against a white sand shoreline. We hurriedly loaded our gear into the unchristened Old Town canoe, a Penobscot 17. Seventeen feet long. I returned the Jeep to the old green house and walked back down to the launch, where I let out a war whoop of excitement as soon as I saw Chris. He was joining me for the first part of the trip, down the Suwannee River to Suwannee River State Park. Chris posed for a picture. Then it was time to head south.

We needed to get moving now to beat the oncoming dark. A strong wind, chilly air, and leafless, barren trees accentuated the wintry aspect of the day. Our paddling was steady in the brand new craft. I was immediately impressed with the stability of the heavily loaded green canoe. Soon the smooth polished wood of the paddle handle felt natural in my hands. The muscles in my back and arms tensed as I dipped the blade into the water and pulled it backward, watching the water swirl and curve after each stroke. I listened for the repetitive pitter-patter of dripping water on the surface of the Suwannee between strokes.

Paddling: self-propelled travel. Once the propriety of Indians from the Arctic to the Everglades, paddling had gone from being a primary means of travel to a recreation and exercise pastime. I had first picked up a paddle on the Spring River in the Ozark Mountains, where my family had gone on vacation. My three older brothers and I plied clunky aluminum Grumman models, negotiating mostly mild rapids between long crystal pools flanked by wooded hillsides, fishing for rainbow trout and smallmouth bass. For some forgotten reason I had sat in the rear of the canoe, steering with a battered wooden paddle, hitting more than a few rocks on moderate rapids, not caring if I tipped us over with the summer Arkansas sun bearing down overhead.

As we grew older and my brothers moved away, the Spring River vacations fell out of favor in our home in Memphis, Tennessee. I did most of my growing up in suburbia, living in the same house from birth to high school graduation, not knowing or caring about much outside my world of sports, school, and socializing. For me, the '70s were a good time to be a kid.

Nineteen-eighty came along and I went off to college at the University of Tennessee—in-state tuition, you know. At UT I fell happily into a typical college life centered on having fun broken by only enough classes and studying to keep the dollars flowing from home. But after two years, I realized I was wasting my parents' money and my own time. It would be better to devote myself to full-time recreation. I had had the good fortune of meeting Calvin Milam, from Chattanooga, a fellow who loved the outdoors, especially the Smoky Mountains. We hung out in bars but also in the nearby Smoky Mountains, hiking and backpacking. I had come to college a completely televisionized, commercialized, homogenized flatlander, oblivious to the outdoors. My trips to the mountains began to color the world differently. I came to see life in nature's terms—a slow-moving evolution of the fittest, everything with reason and purpose, regardless of whether I was there to appreciate it or not. Soon I reveled in being out there, where the busy rush of workaday surroundings faded, the sun became my clock, the dark green tree canopy became my roof, and I had clear streams for plumbing. The physical challenge of walking up and down mountains with my house on my back filled a void left since my sports days.

Meanwhile, I resumed going to school on my own dime and earned an economics degree from the University of Tennessee. By then, my values had changed. I had come to believe, as I still do, that time, not money, is the most valuable commodity on earth. Going off hiking in the backcountry takes *days,* unlike a sport such as tennis, which takes but a few hours per outing. Stringing together multiple days on multiple occasions to satisfy my outdoor craving required lots of free time. To buy the time, I had to sacrifice the opportunity to obtain the quantities of money expected in my middle-class outlook. No "real" job was going to avail me the free time I wanted. To hell with the money, I decided—by now I was camping out upwards of a hundred nights per year.

I had already realized that the "American Dream" of a wife, kids, house, and mortgage wouldn't necessarily satisfy my soul. That route was like a trip on a train—you go down the tracks and have very few places to switch directions. I wanted my life to be more like a hike in the woods, offering plenty of twists and turns, hills and valleys, never knowing exactly where you are but always having an opportunity make your own way without the steel rails keeping you pointed toward one inevitable conclusion.

To fund my outdoor life I continued the occupation that got me through the second portion of college—bartending. It was very convenient. I could work two or three days per week, mostly on weekends, and have enough money to live on. And the weekend work was doubly good—it left my outdoor adventures for the weekdays, when the woods were deserted.

East Tennessee is blessed not only with mountains but also with rivers aplenty. After my friend John Harv Sampley got a canoe, we began to ply the rivers of the area, the Little, the Clinch, the Holston, and the Emory, and my paddling passion was born. We also used Harv's boat, another beat-up old Grumman, for lake paddling trips where we could combine canoeing and camping. We built our skills, dubbing our boat the *River Tamer,* and decided to try the Obed Wild and Scenic River west of Knoxville. The Obed has Class III–IV rapids—nothing so scary that a case of beer couldn't cure. Or so we thought. By the time that spring day was over, Harv had had his shoes torn from his feet and we had flipped numerous times, losing the beer and all our gear except for one paddle. The Grumman had a hole in the bottom and a thwart had been torn from the middle of the boat. We finally gave up and carried the canoe out of the gorge, begging a local farmer to haul us back to Harv's truck. Growing pains.

By this time, my penchant for spending vast amounts of time in the wilds had become fabled among my friends. One pal in particular, John Bland, suggested I write a book about my adventures. I thought about it. I looked at the idea, becoming scared yet intrigued at the possibility. The material was there. Adventures had been had. After some time of contemplation I literally set pen to paper, writing out in longhand a book ultimately titled *Trial by Trail: Backpacking in the Smoky Mountains*. It was a collection of true-life outdoor adventure stories, chronicling my evolution from flatlander to modern-day mountain man.

I was struck by the notion that perhaps I could make a living by writing about the outdoors. It would give my wanderings a purpose and allow me to pursue my passion unabated. That first book led to an association with a publisher of outdoor guidebooks, Menasha Ridge Press, which hired me to write a hiking guide to the Smoky Mountains. Slowly, ever so slowly, especially to those who know the book business, I began to create my job as outdoor writer. The royalties built, but I still had to bartend on the side to make ends meet. I transformed from a bartender who wrote outdoor guidebooks to a writer who bartended on the side and eventually to a full-time writer. Looking back, had I known how long it was going to take, I might never have attempted to craft my slot in the world this way.

After writing numerous guidebooks about places from Colorado to West Virginia to Florida, I still longed to write another adventure book, like *Trial by Trail*. But this time I had to make an adventure happen. So there I was, thirty-nine years old, paddling southbound on the Suwannee River, heading from the suburbs of Memphis to the Smoky Mountains and down to the swamps of Florida.

The Suwannee was surprisingly swift, despite the low flow following the drought. Scarcely an hour had passed before we found a spot to camp, on the inside of a bend beneath a flat of pine and laurel oak, complemented with palmetto. Spanish moss thrived wherever it could find a host. We pulled out the dry bags and hauled them up the narrow sandbar onto the pine-needle-carpeted shelf. I began to organize our stuff again, dissatisfied with the hasty job we had done earlier at the landing.

So there I was, thirty-nine years old, paddling southbound on the Suwannee River, heading from the suburbs of Memphis to the Smoky Mountains and down to the swamps of Florida.

Chris stood over a pungent pine fire he had started. The heart of pine burned brightly. In pioneer days, heart of pine was known as fatwood and was used for torches. We had a gas lantern hanging from a nearby pine limb functioning as our torch. Chris turned his head and asked the Question, the same question so many others had asked me: "Why are you doing this?"

"Why am I doing this?" I repeated, buying a little time, as if I hadn't thought about it enough already. "Strictly speaking my aim is to paddle from right here in Georgia down to the Keys. But I guess that doesn't answer why." To see what's around the next bend, I thought. To go where I have never been, to see something I've never seen. To see Florida from a watery point of view, to ride the river that the steamboats chugged, to paddle the coastline where rumrunners landed their booze, to camp where the Calusa beached their dugout canoes, to see where Flagler ran his railroad.

Chris's question rang in my head, raising more questions. Was I trying to find historic Florida or was this a quest to learn more about myself? Adventure? Face it—for serious adventure I'd probably have to go somewhere so inhospitable, like Antarctica or northern Canada, somewhere so forsaken that I'd likely be killed, and I'd need a sponsor to pay for it. Answers came forth as cryptically as questions.

The moment passed. "Maybe just to pay old Lem ten bucks and hope his ribs stitch up by spring. Maybe I don't really know, but maybe I will when I get there."

2 *Down the Suwannee*

Frost covered the gunnels of the canoe as I walked down to fetch river water for morning coffee. Chris had gotten up at 6:00 A.M. and rekindled the fire. The flickering flames stirred me from dark slumber. After coffee and a filling breakfast of French toast, we once again packed our supplies into rubber-coated dry bags to keep them dry in the unlikely event of the canoe tipping over.

These rubber-coated bags were part of my gear. Gear often defines outdoor adventurers. Who has the most gear? Who has the best gear? Some people are collectors of gear—I call them gearheads. Over the course of two decades of outdoor adventuring I had refined my taste and needs for equipment. The resulting assortment was not as much as you might expect, since I was well along the gear curve. When starting out, people often buy all sorts of stuff, and much of it doesn't work too well or doesn't meet their needs. Longtime paddlers often end up taking along less gear than when they started. Still, our Old Town was pretty full. We had two coolers, one to keep things cool, though that wasn't needed on this trip, and the other, larger cooler functioning as the grub box. Both coolers doubled as camp seats. The dry bags are coated rubber bags sealed at the top by being folded and clipped shut. In those were a sleeping bag, sleeping pad, spare clothes, lantern, cook kit, and tent. Chris had his own dry bag with sleeping bag and clothes. My entire clothes collection, including what I was wearing, amounted to a ball cap, two bandannas, two short-sleeved T-shirts, one long-sleeved button-up shirt, a fleece vest, rain jacket, belt, khaki pants, short pants, rain pants, three pairs of socks, leather deck shoes, and a pair of flip-flops. This trip wasn't about being a clotheshorse; wearing the same thing over and over eliminates decisions about what to wear. In a smaller dry bag was my camera. Yet another bag had maps, books, and notebooks. An immediately accessible bag held sunscreen, bug lotion, radio, cigars, and lighter.

I had two brand new, handcrafted wooden Old Town paddles for us. At later points these paddles might become instruments of torture, but for now they were nice and felt ideal upon the first stroke. Smart paddlers carry an extra paddle, but I lived what one friend called the "personal fable": the belief that nothing bad will ever happen to you. Car wrecks and losing paddles are things that always happen to other people. He was right; I believed in my own personal fable, though it would be tested down the line.

Chris and I were soon on the water, heading down the Suwannee, seeing what lay beyond each bend. The river kept its endless push for gravity between gum trees that flanked the Suwannee. Thin, weak-looking limbs emanated from their squat trunks. The smallish limbs were a result of periodic flooding that pruned back these trees, also known as tupelo. Their trunks grew bigger and bigger, distorting grotesquely. Below, the snakelike roots twisted and turned and writhed over and under one another, resembling a den of snakes descending into the water upon which we floated. While the gums struggled, the stately cypresses grew symmetrically skyward, each trunk thinning gracefully into light sky. Like those of the gums, cypress limbs are short, but they are rigid and strong, less likely to break off in high water. Cypress is prized for construction due to its resistance to rot. It ranges in swampy places all over Florida to Texas, to Delaware, and up the Mississippi River Valley to Indiana. The shapes and sizes of the streamside trees held our attention as we fancied them to be things other than trees, like seeing shapes in passing clouds overhead.

The sandy floor of the river was visible in the shallows. This sugar-white sand and the tannin-stained waters gave the Suwannee a burgundy tint. William Bartram, while exploring the South in 1774, described the Suwannee as the cleanest river he had ever seen, "almost as transparent as the air we breathe." I wonder what he would think about the Suwannee now, still transparent but adorned with occasional aluminum cans and plastic bottles. Unfortunately, like any river, this one catches all that is deposited into its watershed. A can blown from the bed of a moving truck onto the side of a road winds up in a small, dry creekbed. When a big rain comes, the can is dispatched down the creek into the main river. The can gets caught in an eddy. The water recedes, and the can is left high and dry on the riverbank for all to see.

The Suwannee here twisted, turned, and was broken up in places by islands, though still thirty feet or less in width. Trotlines were strung from limbs on the edges of the river. When were they baited and checked? If we drifted too close we risked arguing with a metal hook. The high banks of palmetto and pine were doubled as they reflected from the still waters. Al Griffis had waxed lyrical about his backyard river in the various seasons. We would know only winter on this trip. It certainly had its moments. A picturesque scene opened just beyond a particularly sharp bend. We heard a crashing, splashing noise and looked at each other quizzically. Five or six deer were crossing a shallow section of the river, their legs noisily thrashing through the water. We drifted forward, hoping to remain undetected. Upon seeing us, they bounded up the riverbank with a little more spring in their step, dripping water as they melded into the riverside forest.

Later that afternoon we came to a railroad trestle, the first trestle of many we would see on the trip. A friendly conductor waved upriver at us. We hailed him back with a wave of the paddles. A road span paralleled the track. Once upon a time, the mighty Suwannee itself was the transportation backbone of the area, the highway of progress, if you will. Then the railroad came. Then the cars came. These new modes of transportation had each offered the promise of a richer future for the area. Now the Suwannee River was an escape route back to nature for a few, but mostly it was crossed with a quick glance out of the car window by some passenger absently wondering where that water went.

The spans temporarily shaded the river. Fargo, Georgia, a crossroads hamlet, lay just to the north. We never saw the place—when paddling a river you are on the downside looking up and can't see too far beyond the riverbanks. A limited view really changes your perspective.

Evening came. Chris and I searched for a place to camp, finally finding one atop a steep sandbar on the inside of a bend. A live oak tree commanded the apex of the sand hill, flanked by a row of tall pine. Find any picture of the Suwannee River and you will see in it a live oak draped with Spanish moss somewhere along the river's edge. This stately tree with widespread arms is associated not only with the Suwannee but with the entire state of Florida, from the Panhandle to the Keys. Beyond state borders it ranges west to Texas and along the Atlantic Coast into southeast Virginia. The evergreen foliage gives the live oak its name.

The evening sun retreated behind the curve of the earth. A chill fell on southern Georgia. The temperature dropped to 40 degrees by 6:00 P.M. The full moon illuminated a sandbar across from us as the Suwannee flowed silently. Hunting dogs roamed the woods in the distance, occasionally yelping, their barks sometimes followed by gunfire. Al had mentioned that it was the last weekend of the deer season.

We sat by the fire, tossing broken pieces of pine into the flames, watching the heartwood burst forth light into our camp, and rearranging the coals now and then with a convenient stick. I looked across at Chris. How we had met was, naturally, natural. Earlier wanderings had taken me on a couple of summer-long trips out West, backpacking and generally seeing what was out there. Using time I had bought. I happened on the Gila Wilderness, in southwestern New Mexico, and came to love the place. Some years later I arrived at the Gila for a twelve-day backpacking trip, solo. On a fork of the Gila River I came upon a place called Jordan Hot Springs. It was on the map. The trail took me right by the primary spring, the one where people came to bathe and relax. A man and his son were lounging in the spring. We got talking and they told me they were from Jacksonville, Florida, of all places. I told them I was from Tennessee and had come out to hike, fish, and explore. The man, Bob Phillips, challenged me in a roundabout way to catch a little supper for them. I said I would, if they cleaned the fish. We would all camp out together and have a little fish fry. I proceeded to toss a line up the creek, returning with an armload of smallmouth bass and trout. Around the fire that night we talked in a way that strangers ordinarily don't but people who meet in the outdoors often do. Bob's son was Chris, who had an artistic eye and a love of the outdoor life. The next day we parted ways.

Fast-forward a year to when I was writing a hiking book about Florida's national forests, and as part of the work I was checking out the trails of the Ocala National Forest. Chris was enrolled at Florida School for the Arts in nearby Palatka. I called him and invited him to join me for some hiking and camping. We had a good time, as Chris brought along a few of his buddies from the school, including one Aaron Marable. Chris's dad Bob joined us for one campout too. I admired Chris's enthusiasm for the outdoors and became a mentor of sorts to him. Later, Chris, Aaron, and I took other trips together, ultimately leading to Chris joining me for part of this adventure.

Chris's passion for art matched his enthusiasm for the outdoors. By the time he and I set out in the Old Town he had graduated from Florida School for the Arts and was enrolled at another art school, in Boston. At twenty-three, black hair cropped close, brown eyes dancing around, taking in the scenery, Chris had a mindset ready to take on the world. Sculpture was his specialty. He was facing the challenge of all artists: how to get paid for his work. I thought about the road I had taken—if you can arrange your life to get paid for doing what you love, it makes going to work a lot easier. So many people feel trapped in jobs they dislike because of having built up debt buying things that were supposed to make them happy and then needing to work more to pay for those things. A new car may make the commute more tolerable, but it doesn't make the work any more satisfying.

Putting out art was like putting out a book—a public risk. It could be rejected. Or worse, ignored. But if he didn't try, he would never know. Many prefer not to take that chance; not to lay work on the line or let it "hang out there," as Chris would say—just throw it out, and let the pieces fall where they may. His situation was similar to my Florida trip as a whole, a challenge, a raising of the bar, to see if I could do something I'd never done, go somewhere I'd never been. There was a chance I might not make it. Risk has its thrills, not knowing what lies ahead. Question: If someone could hand you an envelope containing your complete life story from this point forward, would you open it? Would you want to live life if you knew the outcome? That is precisely what makes life exciting—you don't know what is going to happen. We don't know what's around the bend or out in the Gulf of Mexico.

I want to enjoy the moment, not waiting till a series of things happen that will then make me happy. I want to smell the fire, feel the cold wind numb my fingers as they guide the paddle through the water. I want to see five deer swim across the Suwannee River. I want to use my senses, be in the game, be in life.

We lay beside the campfire until the embers were nearly burned out. The moonlight played havoc with my slumber, beaming through between fast-moving clouds. The white orb arched across the sky, my glow-in-the-dark clock. It's hard to hold anything against the cycling beacon of the night when it casts eerie shadows among the trees and softly illuminates the landscape.

I was awakened by the morning cold. My feet were numb. Finally, enough was enough: It was time to start the fire. The hot coals gave way to yellow flames. My tingling toes came back to life with the crackle of burning pine. Our water bottles were mostly frozen. I walked down to the canoe, crunching the icy sand, coffee in hand, and checked the temperature. Twenty-five degrees. The Florida Keys seemed very far away. I returned to camp and made a little breakfast. Shortly, Chris and I set off on the shady river. We were anxious for the sun to rise above the trees and deliver some heat. The wood ducks plying the river edges seemed to enjoy the cool weather but not our presence. Every time they saw us they would take wing with a lot of squawking. I wouldn't blame a wood duck for being a little paranoid; these multicolored fowl were hunted nearly to extinction a century ago. But they have since rebounded and now enjoy a population of over a million.

The river was quiet, save for a hissing over exposed roots on the outside of bends, bubbling and frothing, as if to gain attention. Jets streaked silently high overhead, leaving white contrails slicing the cobalt sky. Sometimes we could hear cars, just a weak rumble in the distance, coming from who knew where and going to who knew where else. I wasn't pretending we were out in the middle of nowhere—just searching for the sense of that. And getting it, most of the time.

Thomas Creek roughly marked the Georgia-Florida border. The slim stream gurgled noisily over the limestone at its mouth. The exact border between Florida and its northern neighbor had been a point of contention for a long time. European powers fighting over North America never set an exact boundary as Florida changed hands. England recognized Spain's border claim at 30 degrees, 38 minutes north latitude, which was later changed to the 30th parallel. The settlers and Indians knew it belonged to whoever dared stake a claim in the untamed land.

Further complicating matters after 1776 was the Spaniards' practice of harboring runaway slaves, headed south from Georgia and South Carolina. The southern planters of a new United States wanted Spain out of Florida, but the Federalists in Congress decided to ease tensions by surveying the exact Georgia-Florida boundary, so that owners could retrieve slaves still on American soil. In 1790, Andrew Ellicott was sent down to mark the line but was prevented from completing his mission by hostile Creek Indians. Then, in 1795, Pinckney's Treaty set the boundary at the 31st parallel, with Spanish and American surveyors working out the line as best they could. The Creek Indians were still causing them problems. Florida's western border was finally set at the Perdido River in 1822, after it became a U.S. territory.

We paddled a short distance up canoe-width Thomas Creek and took our morning break. Chris exited the canoe stiffly. He was starting to get what I call canoer's back. This malady strikes infrequent paddlers and comes on like the ache from any new labor that works specific muscle groups. Paddling was what we were doing. It got us downriver.

Downstream, the innumerable twists and turns of the Suwannee made it nearly impossible to know exactly where we were, despite good maps, a compass, and considerable backwoods experience. Side creeks like Thomas Creek offered certain markers. The afternoon ritual of looking for a camp began. The wild card—where are we going to camp tonight? It can strike you strangely if you think about it: you know you are going to camp out, but you don't know where. For most of us, when we are in town we pretty well know when we get up where we are going to bed down.

In the world of canoe camping I had long ago developed a distaste for sandbars, as the little grains work their way into every crevice of your stuff. Sand gets stuck between your toes as it works its way through your socks. It gets in your cooking pot, in your food, in your mouth, culminating in the crunchy sensation when teeth and grains of sand collide, which is rather like biting foil. The sand is scratchy and annoying as you twist around in your sleeping bag.

So I avoided sandbars, although in summer they would be preferred camping grounds on the Suwannee, as they would be the least buggy locales. Other places were nixed due to difficult canoe landings. Ideally, we wanted a place where we could easily land the Old Town and beach it to unload. Downriver lay a sandy beach backed by a high hammock of live oaks. The word *hammock* is derived from the Indian term *hamas,* or "sleeping place." Chris and I carried the gear to our sleeping place beneath the spreading oak limbs and set up camp.

The day had warmed to nearly 70 degrees. I stretched—a preventative against canoer's back—and gathered a little wood. The temperature dropped at sunset, as is the norm on clear nights. It was time to prepare for another cold one. I erected the tent—the radio said rain was an early morning possibility. After dinner, I set my bedroll near the fire, but not too near, and slipped into the sleeping bag wearing three pairs of socks, pants, two shirts, a fleece vest, a bandanna around my neck, and another over my head. Just about all my clothes at once. You may begin to wonder

Downriver lay a sandy beach backed by a high hammock of live oaks. The word *hammock* is derived from the Indian term *hamas*, or "sleeping place." Chris and I carried the gear to our sleeping place beneath the spreading oak limbs and set up camp.

why I wasn't better prepared. The real problem had been selecting a single sleeping bag for the entire adventure. I needed one warm enough for North Florida and cool enough for the southern reaches. The compromise proved both too warm and too cold. Perhaps conditions would be just right down Tampa way, I thought.

I cinched the top of the bag tight, leaving only a breathing hole. My mouth and nose stuck out from the hole, keeping that life-giving air flowing while I slumbered. Hours later, I awoke feeling like a mummy in a microwave. The warm front had moved in early from the southwest, and the temperature had shot up. My immediate concern was the raindrops now falling on the sleeping bag. I freed myself from the hot prison and threw the fly on the tent.

Chris groggily retrieved gear lying around the camp and stuffed it into the dry bags. The pitter-patter on the oak leaves picked up. We took our sleeping bags into the tent, where the wet drumming on the tent fly quickly sent us back to sleep.

Dawn crept into our plastic abode. Water dripped from the trees, and all was soaked as we emerged from the shelter. Surprisingly, the fire still harbored a few hot coals. I rekindled it, made some coffee, and surveyed our surroundings. It was nearly T-shirt weather, a far cry from the night before. Threatening skies foretold more rain, and soon light drizzle began to fall into the pancake batter. There we were, sitting around a campfire, cooking breakfast in the rain. Not your average Monday morning. I watched water drip into the batter browning in the frying pan. After our water-soaked repast, the rain came on hard, prompting me to climb the sand dune between our camp and the river to look down to see if the Suwannee had risen. The canoe was in the middle of the river, lodged against a submerged tree. When the rain had hit in the middle of the night, I had run down to the water and pulled the canoe far up the sandbar to keep it from floating away if the river rose. Before breakfast, I had walked down and returned the boat to the river, obviously a little too close.

I rushed to the water's edge, hurriedly took off my shoes, socks, and rain pants, and throwing modesty aside, waded naked from the waist down into the dark waters. It was cold, to be sure, but it wasn't like the leg-numbing waters of a mountain stream in my native stomping grounds. I padded over river-bottom debris, carefully threading through a tangle of logs and limbs threatening to trap my legs. The main channel lay between me and the canoe. I edged forward as the waters rose to above my belly button. How deep was it going to get before I reached the canoe? I pulled my shirt and jacket up to my neck. The water crested at mid-chest by the time I reached the canoe. I dislodged the boat from the tree, slung myself over the gunnel, grabbed a paddle from the bottom of the craft, and returned to the sandbar, dripping river water into the boat. Though there was no one to witness this performance, I imagined the canoe rescue to have been quite a diverting sight.

I secured the canoe at the water's edge, dressed, and returned to camp. Soon the Old Town was off on its way, this time with us in it. We slipped down the eerie waterway in a chilly fog, overhung by a blanket of clouds. Limestone cliffs rose from the dark river. In some places, the limestone had eroded into grottoes, even small caves. Occasional riffles in the river sped our progress. We soon passed under State Route 6 as the morning fog melted away. A funny thing about a bridge is that when you are going over it, you never give a thought to whether it will hold up, but when you are going under it, you hope it will stay up during your passage, especially when a car or train is passing over it.

Griffis Camp was thirty-nine miles upriver.

We pulled over just beyond the bridge to take a break. I walked along a sandy stretch of shoreline, finding a cypress stump that looked like a chair. I sat down, basking in a sliver of sun, when something caught my eye. A pair of kingfishers darted overhead, playing chase in the drizzly sky. These pigeon-sized birds are known for hunting along waterways. They perch conspicuously on limbs over the water. Upon spotting potential prey, a kingfisher hovers over the water then plunges in, pulling out dinner more often than not. We continued downriver, pushed by the current. Clouds raced across this sky, outpacing the canoe. The river scenery changed with every bend. Small creeks cut through the high riverbank, forming many waterfalls, first heard, then seen. An afternoon wind began to blow our boat around, forcing us to paddle more steadily than we preferred. Several vultures sat ominously atop a cypress tree, spreading their wings to the sun. I could see why ancient cultures had woven them into the darker side of life.

Rusted pilings were the only relics of Cone Road Bridge. There was a boat landing nearby and, just downriver, a huge alligator.

I walked along a sandy stretch of shoreline, finding a cypress stump that looked like a chair. I sat down, basking in a sliver of sun, when something caught my eye.

The monster must have been at least twelve feet long, but it was docile while lounging in the sun. It was the first 'gator we had seen.

Alligators have long permeated Florida culture. The Spaniards named the reptile *el lagarto,* or "the lizard." In 1791, William Bartram (*Travels*) described the presence of alligators on the St. John's River "in such incredible numbers and so close from shore to shore that it would have been easy to have walked across on their heads had the animals been harmless."

But civilization took its toll on the region's top nonhuman predator, and by the 1940s, alligators were in serious straits. Hunting restrictions were implemented but largely ignored until a total ban on alligator hunting in 1962, which slowed the population decline. Still, poaching was rampant. In 1970, federal law prohibited interstate trafficking in alligator hides, and this, along with reduced demand, nearly eliminated poaching. Even during the population low, however, alligators remained numerous in the most inaccessible areas of the state. It was this population that enabled the rebound of the American alligator that continues today, to the point that it is considered a nuisance in some areas. Though every Florida county has alligators, they are most prevalent in the central and southern parts of the state. They can be found in all kinds of waters, including in phosphate mine settling ponds and occasionally heading into the salty sea. These carnivores start out life eating insects, snails, frogs, and small fish, graduating to bigger fish, turtles, snakes, birds, and small mammals. They eat carrion—dead animals, that is—apparently preferring it to fresh meat.

Since they are so adaptable to human encroachment on their habitat, they can be found on golf courses, in swimming pools, and in drainage ditches. Being opportunistic feeders, some alligators do attack people. But the odds of getting maimed in a car wreck on U.S. Highway 1 are greater than the likelihood of suffering an alligator attack. This rare occurrence always makes the news; the media simply can't resist a 'gator attack. Even as attacks occur, other people are feeding alligators marshmallows or watching them chomp down on fish guts with their menacing jaws. Like bears, some alligators come to associate humans with food and lose their natural fear of two-legged benefactors. In their walnut-sized brains, they can't discriminate between humans with food and those without it. That is why it is against the law to feed wild alligators. The state Game and Fresh Water Fish Commission handles problem alligators. They receive somewhere between eight thousand and ten thousand calls per year about problem alligators in the overall population of more than a million.

One of the reasons we had seen only one alligator was the cold weather. These cold-blooded creatures don't hibernate but go dormant during the winter months, especially in North Florida. A wintering alligator digs a burrow along the riverbank, enlarging the inner chamber so that part of it is above water, and there the animal remains still and quiet, conserving energy.

Alligator meat and skins have been prized by whites for two centuries and for longer yet by Florida's Indians. Hunting has been revived, but commercial harvesting today is done farm-style, where alligators are propagated and raised. This industry now produces 200,000–400,000 pounds of meat and 15,000–20,000 skins per year.

Seeing that giant alligator was the highlight of the afternoon. Then came time to find camp. The high limestone banks, cut in strange grooves, made the job difficult, but persistence paid off when Chris spotted a site on a bluff overlooking a clear tributary of the Suwannee. I guided the craft to a small rock outcrop. Chris jumped out of the boat and I followed. We started to pull the loaded canoe away from the river's edge onto the rock slope landing, straining with all our might. My feet gave way on the slippery limestone, and my legs shot out from under me. I fell directly onto my back, knocking breath from lungs. I looked up with eyes the size of saucers and Chris burst into laughter. So did I, after sucking in some air.

We carefully toted our gear away from the river into a hammock of oaks. This place was once a community called Needmore. The name may tell us why Needmore was no more. From our bluff, we could look over the Suwannee and the clear stream, which drained a swamp upstream. I explored Needmore, seeing some little yellow signs indicating that this turf was now part of the Suwannee River Water Management District, one of the state's five water management districts, which are divided along hydrological lines or watersheds rather than along political lines. Under the delega-

Then came time to find camp. The high limestone banks, cut in strange grooves, made the job difficult, but persistence paid off.

tion of the Florida Legislature, the districts focus on water supply and quality, flood protection, and preserving natural water systems. They balance on a tightrope held at one end by environmentalists and at the other end by thirsty new residents, vying for a share of the water. In Florida, water is power.

The folks of Needmore probably didn't need more water, likely drawing their aqua directly from the Suwannee. But they had found better places to live. The walk around the ghost town, now amounting only to some woods laced with sandy old roads, was a welcome change as I stretched my legs and gave my arms a break.

"We're in Needmore," I reported to Chris.

"You mean people lived here?"

"Yep. When settlers drifted down here from Georgia, they found the soils not quite as productive down here as up there. Too

much sand, too much limestone. In other places cotton plantations thrived, but if the settler picked the wrong spot, it meant
small crop yields, then it got worse. It must've been marginal here
at Needmore."

Chris had grown up near St. Augustine, the oldest city in
America. The coasts of Florida were settled first. Interior Florida
remained a howling wilderness, largely unexplored by colonists
for another three hundred years. Only after Florida became a territory in the 1820s did the interior begin to be a focus for settlement.
It is strange how a wild place, like Needmore, can be settled and
then revert to wildness.

The temperature dropped as darkness enveloped Needmore. I
cocooned myself in my bag, exposing only the air passages. Getting used to this method had taken years of camping out in cold
weather. If you are claustrophobic, forget it. Snugging the material
around my face had the added benefit of dimming bright moonlight, which tends to keep me awake when out in the open. No rain
showers or other surprises bothered us that night.

Chris started a predawn fire and we watched the early morning
show. It was much better than the any show on television. The
moon opened the show, descending into the twisted arms of the
oaks. The ball of pale light slowly turned yellow, then orange, then
blood red, before going beyond the horizon. Dawn was just back-
stage now, emerging from the curtain of darkness. The horizon
colored our neck of the woods nearly in reverse, blood red light
splitting through the pines, turning orange, then yellow, then
white. By full morning we had eaten breakfast and were once
again loading the canoe. Again the water in the bottom of the canoe was frozen. My Tennessee friends, jealous of my long sojourn
in the Sunshine State, would have been laughing at me now. This
was winter camping, despite the latitude.

The limestone outcropping where we had left the canoe was, in
some places, more like soil than rock, as if the rock hadn't hard-

ened yet, like unsettled concrete. It clung to the soles of our shoes and then dried hard, like finished concrete. Such is the nature of "rock" in this part of Florida.

Cool hands were made colder by the hardwood of the paddle. On the Suwannee, we resumed watching the parade of cypress trees that lined much of the river. Cypresses have unusual "knees" that project from the tree's root system above the water. Their significance is a mystery but many think the knees help the tree to "breathe." Around some of the trees there may be up to fifty of these spires. Cypress knees evoke a series of skyscrapers, each trying to outdo the next in height and design. The imaginative eye sees castles or stalagmites.

I saw a few "For Sale" signs posted on lands around us. I couldn't help but wonder what the river would look like in a few years or a few decades from now. Would there be more Needmores? More likely not. I was glad to be able to strip naked at a moment's notice to retrieve the canoe and not have to worry about anyone watching from a kitchen window.

3   *Springs Aplenty*

Occasional palms and magnolias were the only hints we might be down Florida way. Palm trees have long been associated with the usually balmy Florida climate. Eight varieties of palms are native to the state. The sabal, or cabbage, palm is the most widespread. It was designated the state tree in 1953. Initially the royal palm was chosen by the state legislature because of its towering stature and regal appearance, but at the urging of the Florida Federation of Garden Clubs, the more ubiquitous sabal won out in the end.

Palms are unusual in the tree world, having no bark. Instead, they have an outer shell and an inner cylinder, both of which are living tissue. Palms are unbranched and grow from a single bud. When they grow, the living tissue at the center of the palm grows, not shedding or replacing an outer layer, as do other trees.

The riverside magnolias were southern magnolias. This symbol of the South blooms with large creamy flowers in spring and early summer. Their fragrance is arresting. A tall one grew in front of my parents' house, and as a child, I remember coming home and being overwhelmed by the perfume after my mother had picked some blooms and brought them indoors. The native range of this widely planted evergreen lies along a band from eastern North Carolina to Central Florida and west to eastern Texas, and the tree is widely propagated all the way to Venice Beach in Southern California.

The sabal palm and the magnolia were proving, despite being true southerners, that they could withstand cold weather. So were we. But the otter that popped its head above the surface didn't stay long in the frozen air. I think it popped up to laugh at us, judging by what looked like a smile on its face. It was a river otter, perhaps the most playful animal around. Found around fresh water throughout the state except in the Keys, otters wrestle and chase each other, toss and dive for rocks, and repeatedly release and recapture their live prey—fish, crayfish, water birds, frogs, and even an occasional rabbit. Their silky fur has up to forty thousand hairs per square inch. Well adapted for life around water, the otter can close its ears and nose, then swim with its webbed feet and long tail. It has the acute sight of a hunter and makes chase with eyes wide open underwater, directly pursuing fish. In murky water it uses its sensitive whisker hairs to detect fish movement.

More strokes and a few twists and turns took us to a sign nailed to a tree: "Warning, Dangerous Shoals, ¼ mile ahead." "Big Shoals," I said absently. Chris and I paddled forward, the sun in our eyes and the wind at our backs. Soon there was another sign, "Warning, Dangerous Shoals, 500 feet ahead." The crashing water was audible by now. Soon I could see the stairstep drop of the Suwannee. Big Shoals was indeed big, not only the biggest rapid in Florida but a pretty big rapid for anywhere. It makes a double drop that flows over an exposed limestone rampart spanning the river. The first drop falls three feet or so, followed by a good four- or five-foot spill. Below the final drop the Suwannee froths and spits yellowy white foam as it speeds down to a wide stretch that churns and roils below the quiet surface. People often think that foam on a river is pollution. Not necessarily true. The foam below Big Shoals is merely organic material in the water being whipped up by the shoals as the water rushes over the rocks. Water levels can change Big Shoals or any other rapid from a fun ride to a dangerous drowning zone. The water was low now, and I considered a sign for a portage on the left. Part of my brain, probably the part receiving signals from my numb fingers, told me to take the portage. The temperature couldn't have been 40 degrees. A spill in the water would be torturous. Another part of my brain said, "Go for it. This is an adventure, remember!"

The adventure part won as the current pushed us forward; there was no going back. We were on the far right side of the river, the portage on the left. Our side was mostly steep limestone. We locked for the rapids, paddling forward, and shot the canoe flawlessly over the first drops ahead of the main falls. We paddled backward furiously into an eddy just above the five-foot drop and hauled the Old Town out to scout the potential chutes, limited by the low water. But even the best chute was too rocky.

Chris and I decided to haul the canoe over the drop on a rope. I took the stern line and Chris grabbed the front one, and we floated and dragged the boat over mossy rock toward faster, deeper water. Soon we were back in the current, cruising past high bluffs that comprised Big Shoals Public Lands. The area is run by the Florida Division of Recreation and Parks, but with no on-site ranger, the land was literally in public hands—for the moment, ours.

The Suwannee moved its fastest for the next few miles, gathering time and again to force its way through rocky narrows, then slowing at wider sections. We shot through Little Shoals and another smaller drop just above the U.S. Highway 41 bridge and a railroad bridge. We drifted into the frigid shadows of the bridges. Cars and trucks banged across the road span. Chris and I decided to make a little supply run, grounding the canoe. We clambered up to the road, where a sign told us we were in White Springs.

We walked toward the edge of town on the side of the road. A cold wind betrayed the sunny afternoon. Luckily for us, Stormorants Grocery was within sight, beyond the line of grass and trees bordering the highway. The aging block structure was well heated and dark. It was obvious that we weren't from around there, but we went about the business of getting some grub and made our way to the counter, where a heavyset fortyish woman in a stained sweatshirt and worn-out face waited to check us out.

"Y'all camping?" she asked. I wondered how she knew; probably by the "eau de campfire" permeating our clothes. In the chill we had been practically lying on top of our campfires.

"Yep. Been out five days."

"You better keep a good fire going tonight," she said, as Chris and I pushed our way out through the creaky doors. Outside the store an old man in a faded green wool coat sat on a bench, warming in the sun and rubbing his ragged whiskers. He squinted our way with wrinkles running clear from his eyes to his ears.

"You boys paddling the river?"

"Yes, sir," I responded. I guess it was obvious. My answer gave him an opening to talk. Probably any answer would have.

"You hadn't hit the actual White Springs yet—it's downriver. Those springs—they're named for the off and on milky color of the water. That color's caused by sulfur underground. These waters have healing properties, you know. Back before there were cars, a little settlement grew up here, around the springs. It was followed by resort hotels, all centered around the upwelling, the spring. But the 1911 fire destroyed most of the town's best hotels. Now, we're just a forgotten Southern town surrounded by a forgotten river."

"Thanks for the information," I replied. I wonder what else he knew about the area.

We soon found a camp not far from White Springs. The low sun made us more decisive about finding camp. Accessing the site required a nearly vertical climb up a fifty-foot sand bank to a pine and oak flat. After hauling our gear up the bank, which warmed us up, I considered the next thing that would warm us—wood. I bashed high and low through palmetto brush, gathering sticks, limbs, branches, and more, considering wood gathering on a larger scale.

Gathering wood for profit, forestry, was a small-time activity in the Sunshine State until the 1900s. Farther north, in the Panhandle, was the site of the first federally owned forest in America. Back in 1828, under orders from President John Quincy Adams, a tract of extraordinary live oaks was purchased near Pensacola. The U.S. Navy needed a protected source of virgin hardwood to build the wooden ships of the day. The evolution of ironclad ships changed warship-building dynamics, lessening the government's need for wooden ships. It became obvious that Florida had vast forests of all types to be harvested for a variety of purposes. The pinelands of Florida were next for the taking, thanks to a new method of using pine for pulpwood. Formerly, only pitch-free trees had been acceptable for pulpwood, which is used in making paper. Alfred Du Pont sent his brother-in-law to scout the South for timberlands suitable for the pulping process. Edward Ball, the brother-in-law, promptly bought the city of Port St. Joe and all the forest around it. The experiment worked and indirectly led to the row cropping for pines so prevalent in the state today. The St. Joe Paper Company now supplies nearly all its own wood needs from its own forests, which it continues to replenish.

Other places were cut over and left behind to burn and erode. The federal government moved in and bought many of the wasted lands, establishing the Ocala, Osceola, and Apalachicola national forests. Numerous state forests were designated, and the Florida Forestry Association was born, promoting wildfire prevention, tree planting, and prescribed burning. Now, with vast population growth, the problems and opportunities have changed in Florida's forests. The luxury of tree farms sprawling over hundreds of thousands of acres is a thing of the past here. Land is limited, making reforestation important, but so is protecting water quality and enhancing wildlife habitat. The forest industry is sensitive to public opinion and tries to minimize the visual impact of tree harvesting and promote public recreation in Florida's forests. Today, 14 million acres of forest land cover Florida, about 40 percent of the state's total land area. In the 1920s, the state was two-thirds forested. Expect that downward trend to continue as people flock to the Sunshine State.

Chris and I hung close to the fire, cooking steaks, baked potatoes, and baked onions. We sure appreciated that Florida wood. At dawn, I peered with one eye through a tiny hole in my sleeping bag. A healthy coating of white frost covered our rubber dry bags. It had been below freezing for a good ten hours or more. "Chris, are you awake?" I ventured.

A muffled "No," came from inside his sleeping bag.

"When are you getting up?"

"After you start the fire," Chris said.

"Are there any coals left?" I asked, trying to get him peer out of his bag.

"I don't know. Why don't you look and see?"

We were having a battle of the bags. This happens when the mercury draws to the bottom of the thermometer. One guy tries to wait out the other, so he won't have to get up and make the fire. The loser is whoever is colder or has the more urgent need to pee.

I was losing. He had gotten up first on most of the cold mornings so far and stoked the fire. He knew he had that leverage as a way for me to do the deed this 20-degree morning. I unzipped the bag into the Florida freeze. On the positive side, I already had on three layers and long pants. All I had to do was put on my frozen shoes and pull on my coat and I was dressed. Red coals were smoking slightly, and getting the fire going was as simple as tossing a few sticks on the coals and puffing a little. The heat was on.

Chris debagged with a big smile and settled in front of the flames.

We rushed around breaking camp, occasionally pausing to warm by the fire. A little doubt crept into my mind. Why was I doing this? I could be at home warmed by a big furnace providing exquisite steam heat in my old abode in Knoxville. For reasons unknown to this architecturally illiterate writer, using steam for heating buildings had fallen out of favor. But my place was around a century old and had the steam heat, wood floors, and woodwork to prove it. Also dirt in the corners. I could have been at home. No one had actually tried to dissuade me from partaking in the adventure. My family had long ago come to understand, or at least to pretend they understood, my preference for the outdoor life that took me out on the wilder side. To go unheard from and unreachable for weeks at a time was par for the course. I wasn't about to take a cell phone. The electronic leash. Many an acquaintance had acted surprised that a cell phone was not part of the gear. Can't we get away from technology even for a minute?

I didn't want to be gotten hold of at a moment's notice or to be able to contact others in such haste. Certainly emergencies can happen, perhaps to others, perhaps to me. But I like to compare the way I travel to how things were for those living a hundred or two hundred years ago. Can you imagine Andrew Jackson reporting in to his wife Rachel back home as he marched to Florida to conquer the Spaniards? I already had so many gear advantages over Jackson and his soldiers. Was a cell phone really necessary? What is necessary? Living in the wilds reveals how little we in fact need. Define need. Think right now about what you absolutely need. The only thing we really need is our next meal and perhaps a little shelter. Wants and desires are another story.

A short but cold paddle took us to Stephen Foster State Park, where an elaborate structure stood beside the river. It was an old springhouse, built in 1906 as part of the White Springs Sanitarium, home of the cure-all waters. Alongside the springhouse were shops, dressing rooms, and doctors' offices. The resort was popular until the 1950s. Later, the area became a state park dedicated to the memory of Stephen Foster, who wrote "Old Folks at Home," the Florida state song. Foster never saw the Suwannee but heard of its beauty, and its name became the title of his most famous composition. Other songs he wrote are "Camptown Races," "Oh, Susanna," and "Jeanie with the Light Brown Hair."

Now the Florida Trail accompanied us on the north bank of the Suwannee. The Florida Trail is a footpath, not fully complete, intended to run the length of the state from the Big Cypress Swamp near Miami to Fort Pickens near Pensacola. Many sections are finished. This section runs from Stephen Foster Park all way to Suwannee River State Park. I had hiked much of the Florida Trail while writing the aforementioned hiking guide to the state's national parks, forests, and preserves. Every now and then we spotted the orange rectangular blazes that mark the trail. Icicles draped from shadowy north-facing limestone outcrops along the river. My hands felt as if they had icicles hanging off them, too. Naked river birch trees with their papery, peeling bark lined the river where the banks sloped more gently down to the Suwannee.

We soon ran into the first identifiable unmarked spring. This one was just a little forgotten flow of warm and sulfury water emerging beneath sun-bleached limestone walls. It anonymously poured forth and melded with the darker Suwannee. Brilliant sandbars over a hundred feet high hung on the insides of bends. Ahead was another nameless spring, which made a forty-foot run to the river from a sinkhole beside the Florida Trail. Chris suggested we pull over and check it out. As I was exploring the sink, a thorn caught my pants, ripping a long tear in the leg. I kept them on anyway, to wear while in North Florida. They would now be useless in bug country, down south. The mosquitoes would be here, too, if it ever warmed up again, which I was beginning to doubt it would. These doubts were borne out that afternoon. The temperature nose-dived again as the sun dipped below the riverbank trees. We soon reached the evening's campsite. It was another good one, from one perspective. I wanted to camp in solitude, away from houses, roads, and other people. We weren't in search of company. Company would come up as it would come up, by the luck of the draw, happenstance, chance, or whatever you prefer to call it.

The campsite had a drawback from another perspective: it was far from the water. Carrying our gear up the steep, wide sand dune to the woods was the last thing we wanted to do after eighteen miles of paddling. But we did it anyway, then scrounged up some wood in the dusk.

The flames were a balm to the night, and warmed us too. "Are you tired?" I asked. Chris lay on his side, curled up like a dog.

"Yeah. Do we have to cook dinner? I just want to go to sleep," Chris complained.

"Well, I don't see any restaurants around," I wisecracked.

"I didn't realize canoeing was so exhausting. I'm not sure what's more sore, my back or my arms. And carrying all that gear up and down these steep sandbars isn't easy either."

I told him he just wasn't used to it. "You had paddler's back, then paddler's arms. Now you've got paddler's body. Soon you will have paddler's mind, then none of it will bother you any more."

After supper, Chris and I slumbered out under the Florida sky, laid out lengthwise beside the fire. Sleep was sporadic, and I peered out now and then, trying to judge the time by the position of the moon in the sky and the dimming of the wood embers.

I thought over the day. Again the Question came to me. Why was I here? To lie cinched up in a synthetic cocoon? No. Perhaps to see the springs boil up from the river's edge, imagining Florida's earliest tourists trekking to the White Springs Sanitarium, bathing in the waters and hoping for a cure. Perhaps because I wanted to go for a few days without sitting in front of a traffic light, waiting for it to change from red to green. Out here, I could go whenever I wanted. The traffic light analogy was no cliché for me. Over time I had developed a hatred for traffic, traffic jams and being stuck in traffic. But who likes traffic? Residents of our major cities have come to accept traffic as part of the price paid for living there. I never did and never will.

I couldn't help comparing what we were doing to the daily demands of "normal" life. Of course, normal life has its advantages—familiarity of surroundings, presence of family and friends, the reassurance of routine. I mentally debated this issue, like other issues while out in the wilds. Chris was company, but I was often alone and would think about something, anything, any subject, from University of Tennessee football to why we are put on this earth. I'm not a fence rider. Most often I come down on a definite side of an issue, whether it be abortion or restoration of the Everglades. However, while debating I try to come up with points supporting both sides of any argument, in an attempt to explore the issue fully and not necessarily justify my own point of view. I believe most people don't allow themselves the time to do this. Others are afraid to be alone with their thoughts. I liken it to mental exercise. Such are the goings-on inside a man's mind inside a sleeping bag just before dawn on a 30-degree morning on the banks of the Suwannee River.

Chris stirred the fire to life without trifle. I asked the time through my peephole. 6:17. I got up and broke the icy crust off the water pot, an old coffee can I use to heat water over the fire. It's smoke blackened now. After some warm liquids, we were soon on our way down the Suwannee, floating to see a different Florida, the relics outside the Magic Kingdom, to see beyond South Beach, beyond the Daytona 500, beyond the toll roads. To strike the wooden blade from a floating boat with a flowing river leading the way, twist by turn, just like Florida's history.

We came to Suwannee Springs early that chilly morning. It also has a springhouse, an old rock structure held together by mortar. It's part of a park managed by the Suwannee River Water Management District. The spring now flows through a window of the old stone springhouse that once rose far above the current level of the river or spring. Steam rose from the spring run as it bubbled into the main river. Downriver we passed under U.S. Highway 129 and came to a canoe livery. Forty or more boats were stacked on the racks and a few more were scattered on a big sandbar. January was the off season. There was no one around, save a cow and some goats standing high on a wooded bluff. Pasture land must have been nearby. Chris found a turtle shell on the bank and decided to collect it as a souvenir. Later that day we spotted a bloated deer carcass floating in the water. The eye above the water stared blankly into space. Chris had no inclination to keep that. It made us think twice about drinking river water. We decided to drink out of the spring runs flowing into the Suwannee, instead of the river itself. As long as the spring runs weren't sulfury. Way upstream, there were no springs, so it had been the Suwannee or nothing. To some, drinking from spring runs was chancy enough. To others, drinking from the tap is too risky. At least we knew the source of our aqua.

Downriver were three live deer paddling across the river, heads bobbing. We silently floated forward as they crossed the deep water. The deer detected our noiseless presence and panicked. They frantically tried to find hoofholds on a nearly vertical limestone bluff. One gave up quickly and swam back across the river to the sandbar from whence they had come. The others finally swam downstream to a more favorable spot, clambering uphill, dashing

We came to Suwannee Springs early that chilly morning. The spring now flows through a window of the old stone springhouse that once rose far above the current level of the river or spring. Steam rose from the spring run as it bubbled into the main river.

into the woods. Chris and I confirmed the spectacle with a wide-eyed look at each other.

The banks of the Suwannee were changing. The vertical limestone occasionally gave way to gently sloping, wooded ground. Cedars graced the riverside, their stiff trunks of reddish brown bark peeling off in long strips. Tight green boughs grew from their rigid limbs. Live oaks overhung the river, lending a certain lushness to the vista, which was near pristine. If I were a deer, I might live here. It was a beautiful stretch. Protected river valleys like this provide habitat for wildlife. But in the long haul, if we want to keep our wildlife populations up, we'll have to establish contiguous wildlife corridors to allow animals to roam between larger tracts where they can continue to live and reproduce.

When two tracts of land are protected but divided by human population, the separation decreases the likelihood that fauna populations will continue to reproduce as effectively as if they were in a space and population the size of both tracts put together. In order to make both protected tracts more vital and productive, a wildlife corridor connecting the two could be kept open, say along a river or creek, availing animals a natural pathway for movement and migration, keeping the gene flow open. The disconnected habitat of the Florida panther has resulted in inbreeding to such an extent that the cats developed their telltale kinked tails and whorls of hair on their backs. Wildlife corridors have been opened for the Florida panther, but they may be too little, too late. Most of the Suwannee River can and does act as a wildlife corridor.

To our right, a surge of water plowed into the river from a break in the limestone bank. It was Horton Spring Run—a strong push of black water emerging from the ground a mile distant. Chris and I explored the woods here, stretching our legs on a piece of the Florida Trail making its way toward Suwannee River State Park, just as we were.

The winter sun gave way to clouds moving in from the northwest. Beyond Horton Spring Run, the wilder river temporarily ended, as houses perched on high river bluffs became more common. Half-built, homemade hunting and fishing camps were sprinkled among more elaborate full-time residences. Nearly every structure had a dock. These ranged from decayed stairways mixed with some strategically placed logs to five-level architectural showplaces, adorned with flags and deck chairs. More than a few homes had slides or incline railways for getting boats up and down the steep banks. It was a collective portrait of American ingenuity at work; no two docks were alike. The way houses used to be before subdivisions, and stores before strip malls.

The private land didn't do much for our camping opportunities. Night was coming on. We passed the Alapaha Spring Rise. The Alapaha River flows south from Georgia as a strong river and then filters underground, leaving a riverbed with some potholes. It re-emerges, say the locals, at this spring. It is a big spring and the Suwannee River widens at the confluence. Nearby Horton Park, run by Hamilton County, was a potential camping spot, but there was no firewood, and State Road 751 was just too close by. We pressed on, eventually finding a spot on the north bank, once again beside the Florida Trail.

Having pulled our gear up the bank, I set up the tent and took a little walk down the Florida Trail. Rain began to fall. I returned to camp to find Chris organizing the gear, preparing for the weather change. I looked down on the Suwannee. Seeing the raindrops making patterns on the water where the river divided around a partially submerged tree, I fell into a kind of trance. I was just sitting there, watching the river flow, like millions of humans and other animals along all the waterways of the world before me—a moment immutable for eons. The river is always flowing, whether we are on it or not, or camping by it, or five hundred miles away.

For thousands of years it has flowed, before our lifetimes, during our lifetimes, and it will keep flowing long after we're gone.

Darkness brought a wet evening of sporadic rain. It was one of those run-to-the-tent, run-from-the-tent, run-to-the-tent affairs. Chris stayed outside, sitting under a big pine that offered a little shelter from the elements. He cooked us a rice mix, a spartan but adequate meal. One of the positive things about rain is that it will send a weary paddler on a long trip to dreamland.

Luckily for us, the rain had quit by daylight. After a few trips up and down the bluff, we were soon paddling into the dreary morning. Dense fog on the water obscured the view; reduced the world to us, the canoe, and the Suwannee.

Miles later we came to Suwannee River State Park and drifted up to the boat launch. I walked to the campground to find a site. It took many long trips to get our gear up to the campground. Outdoor adventuring is always a lot of work, unpaid but infinitely rewarding. We left the boat by the water. Florida did right in preserving this particular area, where the Suwannee and Withlacoochee River meet. It was once the site of Columbus, a thriving farm town situated at the head the navigable part of the Suwannee. Here cotton growers loaded their harvest onto steamboats bound for Cedar Key in the Gulf. Beside the river, a busy sawmill was run by George F. Drew, who later became governor of Florida. A railroad also passed through here, bridging the Suwannee just below the confluence. During the Civil War, both sides realized the importance of this railroad and the bridge, as beef, salt, and sugar were shipped north from the agriculturally rich central part of the state to feed the Rebels. The Confederates built earthworks nearby to protect the bridge, defensive walls of soil to provide cover in battle. But the Graycoats were never challenged as Union troops were stopped north of Columbus at the Battle of Olustee. The earthworks are visible today inside the state park, which was among the first in the Florida park system. Its original three hundred acres were later expanded to the more than eighteen hundred of today.

The cloudy day never beat 50 degrees, though I did warm up under a hot shower. There was no wait as the campground was nearly deserted. I spotted a clothes washer and dryer at the bathhouse and decided to take advantage of them. I shed all my regular clothes, wearing only my rain pants and jacket, and deposited the rest of the duds in the wash, putting in the right amount of change, along with a little box of detergent from a coin-operated machine. The washer began its cycle and I returned to camp. But when I got back to the bathhouse, I found that the washer had stopped in midcycle. I hustled up more change from a fellow camper, and this time the machine completed the job. I was impatient, as a plastic rain outfit is not the warmest or most comfortable attire. The drying cycle went more smoothly, but it took a good two hours before the whole production was complete. I had been on long backpacking and canoeing trips before and was used to wearing less than tidy clothes, but these weren't bad—it had been too cold to sweat. A little camp dirt and fire smoke were the main culprits.

We spent the day exploring on foot and relaxing our tired paddling muscles. I went to the park office and paid the ranger for our campsite. He acted nonchalant when he figured out how we had arrived. On the little campsite registration form was a spot for a car license tag. We were tagless and carless. But that's what people will do—either act all excited, expressing disbelief about your adventure, or act as if your journey were no more exciting than carrying out the garbage.

Later that evening our friend Aaron Marable arrived, Chris's pal from Florida School for the Arts. He was living in Gainesville at the time. Aaron had agreed to meet us here to take Chris back to retrieve my car in Georgia and drive it to Jacksonville, and to bring me supplies for the solo portion of the journey. He rolled in that evening with the goodies, including some hamburgers for us to grill over the fire.

"Have y'all been cold?" Aaron laughingly asked, his eyes darting between Chris and me, looking for an answer he already knew.

"Not as cold as we were last month," said Chris. We had been on a four-day backpacking trip on the Appalachian Trail in Tennessee's Cherokee National Forest. A front had moved in the day we departed, bringing eight inches of snow and subfreezing temperatures for the entire trip. Aaron had had an inadequate sleeping bag and had been cold day and night, especially when the temperature went down to 14 degrees atop Bald Spring Mountain.

"At least it won't be that cold tonight. I've been watching the weather, thinking about y'all chattering in the morning, wondering who was going to get up and make the fire," said Aaron.

"You know us well," Chris replied. "We've been getting up early, though. Did you bring your sketch book?" Both of them carried blank notebooks that they filled when inspired by the great outdoors, indoors, and just about everywhere else. As I have mentioned, Chris was a sculpture man, whereas Aaron was more into drawing.

"Yep," said Aaron. "We'll have to find a place to do art tomorrow." That is what the two of them called it—"do art." I reckon "doing art" covers drawing, painting, and sculpting.

"Just about everybody comments on the walking stick you gave me," I threw in. On his last trip to Tennessee, Aaron had brought me a stick he had found in the Ocala National Forest; he had carved and painted it. He had done such a good job that the stick was now off limits for the trail.

"Y'all ready for a little dinner?" I asked. Both Aaron and Chris nodded. I put on the burgers while Aaron readied the fixings. Chris sat there salivating like a dog. Minutes later we were eating.

"This hamburger is crunchy," said Aaron, who was known to complain about his food.

"Yeah, it is," said Chris, who was known to eat anything in sight. I took a bite. It was crunchy. Sand. The grill must have been sandy and I had failed to clean it off before throwing the burgers on.

"Reminds me of when we were in the Apalachicola National Forest, by Sheep Lake," I said. Chris laughed, knowing where I was going. This was another adventure when we hiked for several days on the Florida Trail in the proximity of Sopchoppy, Florida. Aaron got a bad look on his face as I went on. "Remember that terrible storm we went through? There we were, the three of us stuck under that five by seven tarp, getting soaked on all sides." That night, the rain had been pouring in every direction but up. We later found out that the storm had spawned tornadoes both north and south of us. After the storm had passed, I got up and restarted the fire. We had some coffee and waited for the sun to rise. Already sore from the fifteen-mile hike, and now also wet, Aaron was not in the best frame of mind around that predawn fire after the storm. Then I had passed out breakfast, a foil package of toaster pastries for each of us.

"I can still see Aaron, the firelight flickering on his wet clothes, saying, 'This trip has nearly done me in. The hike about killed me; my pack felt like it weighed a ton, then came the terrible storm. The lightning! So here I sit, trail-worn and weather-beaten. And to top it off, to top it all off, my toaster pastry is *crumbly.*'"

Chris howled with laughter. Aaron got a little testy, remembering how we had chastised him for the wimpiness of his toaster pastry remark. He realized that the story would haunt him the rest of his camping days.

The next morning at Suwannee River State Park was another cold one. We decided to go on a hike to the old Columbus cem-

Before long it was time to shove off, and the two of them were bidding me farewell on the journey.

etery, one of the oldest in the state. Ironic how the dead had out-lived the town, as it were. Later that day Aaron and Chris decided to go canoeing. I was taking the day off from paddling, with many miles still to go on the journey to the Keys. I explored more of the park including the Civil War earthworks, the bridge, and the Lime Sink Run. Aaron made a trip into Live Oak for our dinner supplies. That night we enjoyed another feast and evening of fireside camping camaraderie. If an army travels on its stomach, so does a paddler.

After dinner I lay on the ground, staring into the flickering flames, feeling the pulsing heat of the fire. I wondered about the folks who had settled Columbus, on this very spot so long ago. What fortitude they must have had, facing sacrifice and hardship, venturing on their own into the unknown. They had been willing to risk the life they had for the promise of a better one. I tried to think how many people I knew who were willing to work half that hard—or work at all—to better themselves? How about me? Could I have done it? Sometimes, it seems as if everyone is operating on some sort of lottery mentality, just skating along, counting on a magic number coming up. In the settlement of Florida, people had to be self-sufficient or they couldn't make it. There would be no government help, no handouts. It seemed that the deepest satisfactions, the most rewarding accomplishments of my life, were those for which I had had to work the hardest. When the early Floridians made their life out here, they must have known satisfaction and built up the confidence to handle anything. That can-do attitude, once the heart and soul of the American psyche, is being lost as people relinquish their independence. Government help ultimately undermines the rewards of self-reliance and independence that Washington and Jefferson had in mind when they established this country.

I thought of the adage that those who ignore history are doomed to repeat it. We need to look inward for answers to our problems, not always to the government and others. When a situation arises and you think up a solution, then act on it and solve the problem, you are developing self-confidence to deal with the next problem. The outdoor life has taught me this lesson well: triumph over adversity. When starting a paddle trip you have a goal, to reach a certain distant location. It takes miles of continuous treading over unknown waters. You must keep going until you reach your goal. Shortcuts only get you lost and confused. There is no quick fix. Along the way, there may be rapids to run, wide-open bays to cross, and confusing channels where you must decide the right path. There are scenic sights, rewarding moments. There are headwinds and strong tides to wrestle, moments of doubt as the way seems to be blocked. But you keep on, staying the course, eventually stringing together enough strokes to reach the destination, your goal. Just like life.

In the murky dawn, I one-eyed Chris rekindling the fire. Good. The heavy mercury I carried was showing nearly freezing, and I waited it out in the cozy bag, waited for the liquid metal in the vacuum to expand. Everyone was quiet. We knew the get-together was breaking up.

This is one the worst aspects of being the constant traveler I am—always saying good-bye. Spending six months a year on the road, mostly in the woods and waterways of the Southeast, has its ups and downs. I love saying hello, but I get sick of always saying good-bye. Before long it was time to shove off, and the two of them were bidding me farewell on the journey. Chris and Aaron were a great help, but now it was time to paddle on alone. I would see them again, after the journey was complete.

 *Solo*

The Suwannee widened here, below its confluence with the With-lacoochee. Now that is a great Indian word, *With-la-coo-chee.* It rolls off your tongue like the water does as it exits the Gulf coastal plain, in search of the sea. I paddled on, solo. The first few minutes were a little odd, getting used to the new paddling situation. I fell into it quickly, having done much solo paddling before. The gear was situated farther forward than with Chris in the canoe, to help keep the boat straight, or in trim, as nautical folk say. The Suwannee was now heading south, the way I wanted to go. It had widened to 150 feet or more in places, contrasting greatly with the twenty-foot width at Griffis Landing.

An unexpected shoal downriver announced its presence as it splashed and foamed over limestone. The water sped up the Old Town and I moved the paddle blade to the rear of the boat, to function as a rudder. Out of the corner of my eye I spotted a goat perched high on a rock above the moving water. At first I thought it was fake, until it turned its head. Perhaps wildlife does admire the scenery.

Limestone outcrops jutted above the water in spots. A low roar down the way eclipsed any river noises. It was Interstate 10. When you get on it from the Pacific Coast Highway in Santa Monica, there's a sign calling it the Christopher Columbus Transcontinental Expressway. It runs all the way to Jacksonville, Florida. Every manner of vehicle barreled down it at seventy miles per hour or more, banging and clanging, the racket echoing off the wide river. I'd driven that road many times, hurrying across the land. A long time back, another quieter road traveled this east-west corridor in the Sunshine State, the Federal Road. Florida's first cross-state road was built to connect its two most important cities at the time, Pensacola and St. Augustine. When Florida became a U.S. territory, in 1822, a delegation from St. Augustine made a fifty-nine-day trip by boat around the peninsula to reach Pensacola for the new territory's first legislative session. For the second session, Pensacolans came to St. Augustine. That trip took only twenty-eight days but included a near-fatal shipwreck. During this second session, it was decided that a location halfway between the two cities would be the capital. That way both groups could avoid the harrowing and time-consuming sea voyages. It was still a rough two-week overland journey for each group to reach the selected fields near the former Indian settlement of Tallahassee. In 1826, the Federal Road was built, linking Pensacola to the new capital of Tallahassee. The eastern portion, connecting the new capital to St. Augustine, was called the Bellamy Road, after a prominent planter who built much of the thoroughfare. On I-10, a modern federal road, it's 195 miles between the two cities, a three-hour trip in favorable traffic.

Think about the shape of Florida. Is the state longer or wider? If you guessed wider, you are right. It is 465 miles across at its widest, and 447 miles at its longest. Florida encompasses 54,090 square miles, making it the twenty-second largest state in area. Its

The Suwannee widened here, below its confluence with the Withlacoochee.
I paddled on, solo.

highest point, 345 feet, is in Walton County. The lowest is anywhere bordering the coast. That's where most of the population lives, within a few feet of sea level.

The Suwannee dropped into the coastal plain, heading toward sea level. Resurrection ferns hung green on the horizontal arms of the live oaks towering over the water. These plants are epiphytes, or air plants, that grow on another plant. The recent rains had revived them. Growing mostly on the arms of live oaks, resurrection plants get their name from the way they curl up, shrivel, and turn brownish during dry times, only to roll out and revive, turning green again, "resurrecting," after rain. Epiphytes do not live off the nutrients of their host plant. Instead, they absorb nutrients and moisture from the air and rainfall.

The number of cypress trees declined. The low water revealed more springs than could normally be seen, small nameless springs boiling up along the banks. I came upon a mother raccoon leading a passel of babies, all peering into crevices in the limestone, hunting for a late breakfast. The crew darted into a larger dark crevice after spotting the boat. Wild animals by definition stay away from people. Actually, they are just animals until encountered by humans, who can then call them wild. If an animal is in a forest and no one sees it, is it wild?

Sandbars were fewer now. The few left were mostly covered with grasses. As I neared the town of Dowling Park, some riverside buildings stood over the wooded horizon. One building was five stories high. I couldn't figure out what it was, but I knew I didn't want to be in there on such a pretty day—partly cloudy, upper 60s, no wind—ideal canoeing weather. The bridge at Dowling Park was as decrepit looking as the I-10 bridge was sturdy. It's a good thing drivers don't look under bridges before they go over them. Beside the tired bridge were the broken-up remains of one it had evidently replaced. The wide river reflected sunlight, doubling the brightness of the sky. The Suwannee was a full-blown river now. The afternoon wore on, and the sun made me drowsy. Before I camped the river offered one more surprise—wild turkeys. There must have been twenty or more of them, scratching around on the ground and kicking up leaves at the water's edge. Some Indians considered wild turkeys stupid and cowardly and wouldn't eat them for fear of ingesting these traits. In contrast, Benjamin Franklin admired them and thought them a good choice for our national bird. Turkeys are watchful creatures, often roosting over water for added protection. They are a politically incorrect bunch of birds, the males strutting their stuff with their tails fanned out, cooing temptation to the hens and gobbling insults at other males, each working hard to woo himself a whole harem of delectable mates.

I hauled my gear up another steep bank onto some Suwannee River Water Management District public lands to camp for the night. This up-and-down-the-hill thing was going to keep me in shape whether I liked it or not. As with many another thing that is "good for you," you might not like it while you're doing it, but after it's over you'll be glad you did. I chose a camp away from the river and soon sat before the fire. After another glamorous noodle supper, I lay on my back and looked up through a breach in the live oaks. The moon was rising later now, so the star show was improving in the early dark. The events overhead were and are simply fascinating. Immense nuclear explosions in space, eclipsing one another in intensity, range, and number—brought to us at the speed of light, yet millions of years old. Uncountable worlds, galaxies, holes, and who knows what, behaving in time- and mind-warping ways we can barely understand. How many times had people before me done the same thing? Stargazing with so much less scientific comprehension than I had imbibed, no wonder they invoked myth, folklore, and religion to explain such unfathomable complexities. I did too. It was God's work.

The morning dawned cool and foggy. Weather is almost everything to the outdoor traveler. It sets the tone for the day and greatly affects what is going to happen. It's quite different "out here" when you are out here and staying out here and not going "in there." Weather has a much more commanding effect than when you merely need to know what it will to be like for the forty-three seconds it takes to walk from your house to your car and back again.

The racket of machinery broke the peace and silence on the river. The machines, big trucks and digging behemoths for which I had no name, were working a nearby phosphate mine. The compound has been important to the Florida economy and remains the state's third largest industry today, behind tourism and agriculture. Around fifty thousand jobs are phosphate related, and the industry supplies 75 percent of the nation's total phosphate production. Phosphate was first found in pebbles in the Peace River, but the first mine was in Alachua County, near Hawthorne, in 1883. It was dug by hand, using wheelbarrows, picks, and shovels. Gradually mules, steam shovels, and pumps were added to get to the phosphate ore, which generally lies about fifteen to thirty feet below the surface. Florida prisoners used to work the mines. For a long time the state had no prison for convicts and instead leased them out to private contractors, who paid for the convicts' upkeep, holding state expenses down. Armed guards with lashes kept the workers in check. Abuses resulted, and the practice was ended in 1923 when a prisoner from out of state was killed by an abusive employer. A prison was then built in Raiford.

Nowadays machine-operated draglines strip off the top layers of earth to reach the phosphate-bearing rock. Next the rock is dumped in a pit and high-pressure water guns are turned on it, making a slurry that is then taken to a processing plant. The massive amounts of water needed taxed the aquifer, so the industry now reuses 95 percent of its water. A typical Florida phosphate mine yields ten thousand tons of phosphate rock per acre. Nearly all phosphate is used in fertilizers. But a small portion is used for making common household products such as soft drinks, light bulbs, toothpaste, and shaving cream.

Houses dotted the banks. All sorts of flags were flying: American flags, Rebel flags, University of Florida flags, Florida State University flags, and state of Florida flags. I admire people willing to display their colors and stand for something, whatever that may be. What is now Florida has flown many flags; Pensacola is known as the "City of Flags." The Calusa and Tomoka and other Florida Indians didn't have flags, as far as I know, but since those peoples were dislodged, Florida has flown the Spanish, French, English, American, and Confederate banners. The American flag has added a few stars since it was first flown over Pensacola, St. Augustine, and Tallahassee. Display of the American flag has grown exponentially since the September 11, 2001, terrorist attacks.

Along this stretch, wherever there wasn't a house, there was a "For Sale" sign up. There were so many "For Sale" signs that it seemed the whole riverbank was for sale. Before you imagine Megalopolis by the River, bear in mind that only some of these houses were occupied. The unoccupied ones were weekend getaways or had been abandoned. Every abandoned place had started with someone taking down a "For Sale" sign. They built docks or steps down to the river and put up a wooden building or installed a trailer. Now these were in every stage of disrepair: broken windows, moss-covered sheds, rotted steps, a dock halfway underwater. Half-sunk boats completed the picture. Suwannee River dreams abandoned. Each picture held clues, too few clues, which I couldn't piece together. They left only questions.

Among the ramshackle houses were places that were obviously primary homes, well kept and usually on pilings. I found it hard to imagine how high the Suwannee must rise to reach the stilts on those high banks. Rivers run downhill, seemingly dormant, but when the rains come, the water can turn on those who seek to be near it to enjoy the attractive scenery and recreational opportunities. Water has but one impulse—to seek its level, regardless of what is along its banks. The Suwannee River has the largest drainage basin in Florida, though its headwaters are in Georgia—the Okefenokee Swamp and the Withlacoochee and Alapaha rivers. But 204 of the 230 river miles of the Suwannee proper are in the Sunshine State. The drainage basin of the Apalachicola River is larger overall, primarily the Flint and Chattahoochee rivers, but only a small part of the drainage basin lies in Florida. Not surprisingly, the Suwannee is second to the Apalachicola in average flow. A quarter of the Suwannee's flow comes from its famous springs, making it less susceptible to the water temperature swings that occur in surface rivers. Spring-fed rivers, called calcareous rivers by scientists, are generally clearer, too. The Suwannee starts out burgundy in color from vegetational decay in the Okefenokee, then receives spring input, mostly crystal clear, in its midreaches. Most of the large springs along the Suwannee bubble up clear, and the water keeps its clarity during its short run to the river itself. In contrast, the Aucilla River, south of Tallahassee, starts flowing directly from a spring and is a kind of ultralong spring run, then gets colored a bit in its lower reaches.

A look at my Florida gazetteer showed the Suwannee dividing Suwannee County from Lafayette County. The Suwannee had been dividing counties since it crossed the Georgia line. Florida started with only two huge counties, Duval and Jackson, separated by the Apalachicola River. What is left of Jackson County—named after Andrew Jackson, as was Jacksonville—is just a slight piece where Florida, Georgia, and Alabama meet. Duval County is home to Jacksonville.

Any paddler along the river couldn't help but notice the proliferation of rope swings. Ropes of every color and thickness hung from the limbs of cypress trees, river birch, and overhanging oaks. Some looked ready for a swing and a splash into the water, but the air and aqua were too chilly. And, just like the houses, certain of the swings were of dubious integrity, half broken off or rotting. A few had Spanish moss growing on them.

Beyond the phosphate mine some pine plantations rose in ranks immediately behind the riverside hardwoods. Pine has been important not only for timber and paper but also for turpentining. I had learned about turpentining early in my Florida explorations. You can still see evidence of turpentining on pine trees in older woodlands of the Apalachicola National Forest, St. George Island, and other areas. Look for black, vertical barkless areas with V-shaped scars, each showing where an incision was made in the tree by a galvanized metal gutter, in winter. A container was placed below the gutter. When summer came, resin would flow into the container, known as a "gerty cup," a special kind of clay pot. Resin was poured from the gerty cups into barrels placed in the woods. The barrels would be hauled out by wagon and the pine resin would be distilled into oil of turpentine, which was used for explosives and detergents and in shipbuilding. One person sees a pine tree, while another sees by-products of the said pine tree.

Charles Springs lay "on river left," as paddlers like to say. The springs were too interesting to pass by. Each had its own look. I tied the boat line to a cypress knee and walked back into the woods to where the spring emerged from the ground. Here translucent, sky-blue pools were divided by a small limestone bridge. How these springs were created in the first place goes something like this: As the earth's climate changed over thousands and thousands of years, Florida was repeatedly inundated by an advancing and retreating sea. Each time the land was inundated, marine sediments were compacted, producing layers of rock. When the water retreated, clay and sand of varied depths covered the limestone. Organic acids from plant matter eroded the limestone, creating large cavities in the rock. Fresh water filtered down into the limestone, forming an extensive aquifer system in the upper reaches of the limestone. This is known as the Floridan Aquifer, and is the source of over three hundred major springs in the state, along with countless other smaller springs. The Floridan Aquifer underlies not only all of Florida but also southeastern Georgia, southern South Carolina, and extreme southeast Alabama.

Surface water still filters through porous soils, such as sand, into the aquifer, recharging it and placing pressure on the water already in the aquifer beneath impenetrable confining soils such as clay, creating a "pressure head" so that water is forced out downslope where the confining soil has been broken through. Interestingly, during times of flood, the pressure of rising flood-waters causes many springs to reverse flow. These springs are a window into the Floridan Aquifer. If the springs are polluted, so is the aquifer. Another debate brewing over the aquifer involves concern about drawing it down too much. If the aquifer is drawn down too far, there is less pressure from the fresh water to keep sea water at bay. Seawater encroachment on the aquifer would be disastrous. Water always seeks its level, whether salt or fresh.

Charles Springs flowed down a short run into the Suwannee River. I pulled up to a beach where the run met the Suwannee. The springs are named for Ruben and Rebecca Charles, the first permanent European residents of Suwannee County. By the 1820s, they were running a trading post and operating a ferry on the river. During the Seminole Wars, the United States established a fort near the ford to protect the ferry. Today, the springs are part of the Suwannee County park system. Just as I came back to the canoe, a father and son were drifting down the river in a johnboat. The father, around thirty-five, was patiently trying to teach his excited son to fly fish. I listened to their interchange and wished for the kid to do well; also for the father to develop all patience he could. Fly-fishing is difficult for anyone, much less an eight-year-old kid.

Beyond Charles Springs the first motorboat of the trip grumbled past me. The bluish white smoke from the two-stroke engine was a new scent, and not pleasant. The friendly pilot was checking his trotlines. He asked where I was going, where I had started, and where I was from. These were the three primary questions asked of me all along the river. I answered pleasantly and prepared to answer the questions many more times.

Four canoes full of kids and counselors from a camp pulled away from Blue Springs. They were wildly eager as they debarked from the ramp there—talking and shouting and generally enjoying the day. Their enthusiasm was admirable. But as they passed my camp later that afternoon they were silent. The reality of stroke after stroke after stroke of the paddle had already set in. I don't know whether they kept going far enough for canoer's back to kick in. As they passed, I began to calculate just how many strokes it would take me to get from the Okefenokee Swamp to the Keys. Assuming I paddle five strokes per minute, multiply five by sixty minutes. That's 300 strokes per hour. Multiply 300 by seven hours of paddling per day, and you get 2,100 strokes per day. Take off 100 strokes for slacking off, and make it an even 2,000 strokes per day. Now multiply that by sixty—the number of days I figured it would take to reach the Keys. That made a grand total of 120,000 strokes. I decided I had better think no more about that.

Shoals surprised me at Telford Springs. I was ever happier that the Suwannee River was low. The 120,000 strokes seemed a few less now, as the shoals pushed me toward the salt water. There were more limestone outcrops, more springs, and more shoals to send me downriver and break up the 2,000 strokes of that day. Ahead, the Florida 51 bridge was a miniature Golden Gate span— suspension cables anchored to abutments on both sides of the river. There were no bridge supports rising from within the river. The myriad ways of bridge construction were unexpected. I figured there was a standard way to build them—just one more example of all the things I don't know and had never considered trying to know. Watercourses had varied banks and soils, possibly accounting for varied construction techniques. Uses, budgets, and a few more things only an engineer would know might also change the picture. This interruption-free span was good for a boater, especially one who was lying in the canoe, absorbing the warmth of the sun, and avoiding a few of the 2,000 strokes of the day. Turtles were sunning on top of exposed logs. I had more in common with the turtles than with the bridge engineers. As the boat neared, the turtles would roll off their logs and drop into the chilly water. The chicken turtle and Suwannee cooter turtle browse on the lush riverine plants. "Stinkjims" or mud turtles are named for their propensity for river bottoms and their unpleasant, musky odor when brought to the surface. A more familiar turtle is America's largest freshwater turtle, the alligator snapper. It is recognized by its long, alligator-like tail and three rows of ridges along the back of its shell.

Most springs were near the river's edge. The land was lower here, resulting in more pressure on what underlying limestone there was. The limestone was thinner here, too, making the aquifer more likely to break through, creating the springs. Running Springs were twin springs, divided by a high bluff and privately owned, as a "No Trespassing" sign declared. I paddled in close, not trespassing, to see the clear blue water. I paddled on.

Just downstream was an old iron bridge unlike any other I had seen. The former railroad bridge had a large cylindrical pylon in the center. Between the pylon and the metal span, where the tracks had been, were wheels. Back when the bridge had been functional, these wheels had allowed the entire span to pivot from its usual location crossing the river to run parallel with the watercourse instead, allowing paddlewheelers with tall smokestacks to pass. The tracks have now been pulled from a railroad that was the second oldest in the state. Anglers were bank fishing in sight of the bridge. I waved to them. One man nodded his head, hands intently on the pole, waiting for a fish to bite.

Just below this spring was an old iron bridge unlike any other I had seen.

I didn't need to paddle much farther to find an appealing camp on a high bank of pine and live oak directly overlooking the river. From the perch I watched day turn into night, not doing too much beyond turning potatoes and onions baking in the coals. What is it about fire that is so mesmerizing? Has it been genetically programmed into us? I snapped out of reverie long enough to enjoy the hot treats, slathered in greasy margarine, and ate like a cave man.

Foggy mornings were becoming the norm. The canoe was drifting downriver, and my mind was drifting all over the place, when the aroma of cow manure wafted across the water and focused my thoughts. Nothing like cow pies to wake you up. Cow pies could replace alarms. A cattle ranch was obviously nearby. It can be said that cattle ranching is Florida's oldest industry. The Spaniards brought cattle here, and the bovines soon took to the prairies of the central part of the state, especially around present-day Alachua County and points south. Soon after the first cattle were imported there were escapes. Wild cattle became part of the early landscape around Lake Okeechobee. Often scrawny, these "yellowhammers" were captured and fattened up before being sent to Cuba and points beyond. During the Civil War, the cattle of Florida were critical to feeding the Rebels. Drovers herded cattle north at rates of up to six hundred animals per week. However, some ranchers were playing both sides, loyal only to the highest bidder. The Union realized the importance of Florida foodstuffs and other re-sources, leading to the Battle of Olustee, the largest Civil War en-gagement in the state. Aiming to starve the Rebels, a Federal force had taken Jacksonville and headed west to cut off Confederacy-bound food supplies from central Florida. Southern forces picked Olustee as a good defensive place, with Ocean Pond on one side and a deep swamp on the other. On February 20, 1864, the oppos-ing armies battled beneath the towering pines until dark, and the Union was forced to retreat eastward to Jacksonville. The South had scored a decisive victory, keeping the meat heading to points north, to their brethren fighting in Virginia.

As Florida's cattle industry grew, the cowmen developed a dis-tinctive way of life. Called "Crackers" for sounds of their whips as they herded the stock, they were the first American cowboys, driving large herds from the central prairies to the east and west coasts, staying in the saddle all day long. At night they settled down to biscuits and salt pork—and swatting mosquitoes. Upon reach-ing a port, such as Punta Rassa, the Crackers would be paid in gold and would let off some steam, shooting their guns and drinking Cuban rum straight from the jug.

By the mid-twentieth century, Florida was a major player in the beef industry. Brahmas and other breeds had been introduced, making each cow meatier than the old yellowhammers. Ranchers still grazed their cattle on the open range. But the advent of the automobile, then roads, and more people driving the roads threatened the old ways for the ranchers, and by 1952 the state enforced fencing along roads. Before this, Florida law gave citizens the right to graze on any open, unfenced lands. Today ranching ways are threatened more by the skyrocketing land values that follow expanding subdivisions, retirement communities, and strip malls.

The riverside cattle ranch gave way to more houses. A sign in front of one house said: "Nude swimming and fishing." I hoped these folks were especially careful around fish hooks, but there was no one around to offer any fuller explanation of the sign advertising the situation. Beside it were a dock and a locked boat—the first boat I'd seen chained to the dock. Perhaps nudists don't trust their fellows. All the boats I'd noticed, from foot-powered pedal boats to fancy speedboats, had simply been tied up at docks, engines and all. The locked boat was an old, faded canoe.

The river headed southeasterly into the morning sun. The heat was welcome—it warmed my bones and melted the fog. Narrow wooded islands split the river in a couple of places. These were the first islands since Georgia. Mild but perceptible shoals saved a few strokes of the paddle. Mockingbirds and cardinals sang out over the river. Buzzards perched in the trees. Ducks swam along the river's edge. Nature was alive. All these birds would have raised the spirits of even the loneliest paddler.

I noticed an upwelling ahead. These could be discerned from a distance as breaches in the riverbank, looking like small coves. I paddled that way: Mearson Spring. A big gar hung still in the water where the clear spring ran into the tea-colored river. Gar are a favorite food of the alligator. This throwback to dinosaur days has a

Downriver, Little River Spring was smaller. It had a short run over a sandy bottom. The waters flowed clear beside a beach at the confluence.

long snout with numerous teeth. The fish are found throughout the state and west to Texas. In sluggish, poorly oxygenated waters gar will breathe air through an air bladder in addition to using their gills. Though gar are not commonly fished for or eaten today, the Seminoles reportedly preferred this fish to other species. The alligator gar is the biggest of the species, sometimes reaching ten feet in length and more than two hundred pounds; the Florida state record is 123 pounds.

I paddled over the vent of Mearson Spring and looked into the depths. It put tiny mountain springs—my idea of springs before the Suwannee experience—to shame. I'd be hiking along a mountain ridge hoping for a little trickle of water dripping from a rock at the head of a hollow, to wet my whistle. A Florida paddler could just pull the whole boat *into* the spring and dip in a cup! On down was Troy Spring, even deeper. This is a first magnitude spring, defined as one that flows at least a hundred cubic feet per second. Visible in its depths is the *Madison,* a Confederate supply ship that was intentionally run aground to keep it from falling into Union hands. The hull of the steamboat points toward the head of the spring.

Steamboats had been plying the river since the late 1830s, carrying agricultural supplies, passengers, and mail along the river. But the heyday of the steamboat was in the decades after the Civil War, for shipping in and out of Columbus, New Troy, and Branford. There were also honeymoon cruises and the like. The first blow to steamboat traffic on the Suwannee was the 1896 Hurricane, which roughed up Cedar Key. Then, as always, efficiency won over romance, and railroads began to handle freight transportation. By the 1920s, the steamboat era was over.

Downriver, Little River Spring was smaller. It had a short run over a sandy bottom. The waters flowed clear beside a beach at the confluence. I landed the canoe and walked around. Mullet schooled about in front of me. These springs were widening the river; it was around 170 feet at this point. Stopping and visiting the springs was a continual treat and broke up the monotony of the paddle. Any long trip has a monotonous element to it, simply because you are repeating an act over and over and over again. Don't let an adventurer lie to you.

By Branford Springs, I had stripped down to hat, sunglasses, and long pants. The sun warmed my pale skin. The setting at these springs was quite different. For starters, it lay in the shadow of U.S. Highway 27, which killed the atmosphere. So much for every spring being such a great experience. A paved riverside parking lot, a scuba/bait shop, and the town of Branford surrounded the actual spring boil. A full-blown tourist trap. Divers would see this spring from a different perspective. Since the first cave spring dive in 1953 at Silver Springs, divers have been mapping the flooded cave systems underlying the state. Among the one hundred mapped miles in Florida are long tunnels and cavities as tall as a ten-story building and hundreds of yards across.

I decided to take advantage of being near Branford, tying the canoe in the shadow of the U.S. 27 bridge. This town was originally called Rowlands Bluff, but when Florida's premier railroad man, Henry Flagler, built a line to this steamboat port, citizens renamed it New Branford after Flagler's Connecticut hometown, later dropping the "New." Back then, most folks admired industrial pioneers and entrepreneurs, realizing that they were the engines driving an economy. Can you imagine a town today renaming itself after a business icon? Not in the era when the word *corporation* is most closely associated with the word *evil*. I don't claim to know all with my degree in economics, but I can't understand why so many fail to grasp that it is the people with money, the rich people, who start businesses and invest in companies. These companies, in seeking profits, create jobs to meet the public need for the product or service they provide. Instead, there is a pervasive resentful attitude toward the wealthy because they are perceived as profiting off the backs of working people. When was the last time someone with no money got you a job?

I left the economic debate down at the river's edge and clambered up the rocks to U.S. 27. The sun felt hotter on the pavement than down on the river. But what shocked me were the gas prices at the local minimart. Good thing the Old Town canoe didn't run on high test. Florida gas taxes were higher than those in Tennessee or Georgia. I went into the minimart, where lunch patrons were silently chomping away. In unison they slowly looked up at the figure walking through the door—then went back to chewing their food. I walked to the back of the store and got two jugs of Diet Coke, paid the bleached blond clerk, and walked back into the sunshine, gratefully heading toward the U.S. 27 bridge. That was enough civilization for me.

While returning to the boat I made eye contact with the driver of a passing hay truck. He waved and I waved back. A spontaneous moment of southern grace. To be friendly for no other reason than to be friendly. May it live forever.

Yep, I'm a Diet Coke drinker. Hot, too. I learned to drink it hot while camping out all the time without benefit of coolers and refrigeration. I'd buy the big ones and drink straight out of the jug. Diet Coke is fizzier when it's hot. Keep in mind that I kept at least a gallon of water per day for slugging, too.

The afternoon steadily warmed up. It was the first day the temperature climbed above 75 degrees. I was actually attempting to paddle in the shade, a far cry from the week before when it had been so cold. Weather! We are always searching for the perfect equilibrium of comfort, not too hot, not too cold. I passed some Suwannee River Water Management District lands, where there were campsites aplenty. My arms said stop, but the sun was still too high in the sky. About an hour later, I came to a stretch of houses. The sun dropped a notch. Finding a camp was becoming a problem. Stopping earlier would have been better. My worn-out paws didn't fancy carrying my gear up a big hill either. So after finding a low flat splitting a high bank a fair distance from any buildings, I told myself: "That looks like camp to me." When you are alone, there is frequently no avoiding conversations with yourself.

The low spot was the runoff floodplain from a swamp behind the bluff. During wetter times water would flow through here. The short gear-carry suited my tired bones, and before long I was stretched out on my pad, giving my back a break before gathering wood. Cedar trees held the higher ground. I scratched up some fallen sticks and enjoyed a most aromatic fire. It had been a twenty-mile day, my first of the trip. Nine hours in the canoe. Two thousand plus strokes. I wasn't in a hurry. Whenever the paddle was getting the better of me, I recalled Roman slaves, powering galleys day after day, with bad water for the palate, thin gruel for energy, and a bucket for a bathroom. Not that I was feeling sorry for myself; far from it.

Looking at the gazetteer, I plotted and planned the next day's run after exploring the woods around the camp. A late evening wind kicked up, so I let the fire die. The after-dinner reading session soon sent to me to sleep, or perhaps it was the paddling. It really didn't matter. I was asleep just the same. Sleep did not accompany me through all the hours of darkness, however. Mosquitoes were biting my head, the only exposed body part. I threw a bandanna over my face, but it fell off and I awoke swatting. And so the cycle went. That had been the advantage of the cold weather the week before—no mosquitoes.

The troublesome "swamp angels" were my morning alarm clock. To think I would be nourishing their future generations! By the way, only female mosquitoes bite. Isn't that just like men, letting the females do all the work? The male is probably back at the homestead watching sports on TV. It was already daylight. I jumped on the morning chores after a little Java and was on the water by 8:00 A.M.

On the water. For Floridians, whether it is being on the water, accessing water, being near the water, or being away from too much water, water has been the primary determining factor in living locations. Now, Florida is being sucked dry as it tries to provide irrigation for millions and millions of people and the needs of their daily lives and businesses. Water was precious for Florida's first residents, too. Based on the dating of artifacts from the Ichetucknee River, archeologists confirm that Indians were in the Suwannee River Valley twelve thousand years ago. They will go back no further. At that time sea levels were much lower than today—

the water was tied up in glaciers up north. Florida was higher, drier, and colder and had twice the land stretching out into what is now the Gulf of Mexico. Groundwater levels were much lower; the swamps, springs, and lakes simply did not exist. Water was hard to come by, but it did gather in the occasional limestone pockets near the surface. It was at these watering holes where not only the Indians but also nature's beasts drank. These beasts provided their food. Beside the waterholes the paleo-Indians camped and lived out their lives. Many of these former waterholes are now in river and spring basins. Archeologists access them by scuba diving for artifacts. Water has preserved artifacts in wood, bones, and even plants that would have decayed in the earth.

Fast-forward twelve thousand years, and it was water that saved Florida's last free-roaming Indians from extermination. Vast amounts of water. The sweeping flow of the Everglades and the density and depth of Big Cypress Swamp were too taxing on the federal soldiers who pursued Florida's remaining Indians in the mid-1800s, finally leaving them to their watery refuge, where they formed the nucleus of today's Miccosukee and Seminole tribes.

Fast forward a few more years to a state of 16 million souls and a lone paddler seeking historic Florida on a warm winter morn. I came to the confluence with the Santa Fe River. High banks of feathery pines stood to my right with more swampy terrain where the two rivers met. The Santa Fe was dead ahead—meeting the Suwannee on a collision course. The Ichetucknee flowed into the Santa Fe a little way upstream. The Santa Fe and Suwannee waters melded, the more voluminous flow of the Suwannee coloring the ultraclear waters of the Santa Fe until the two rivers became one. I was 60 miles from the Gulf and 170 miles downstream from Griffis Camp back Georgia way.

There was a Spanish mission here in the 1600s, near the confluence. Besides finding gold and treasures, Spain wanted to convert Indians to Christianity. With this in mind, friars set up a series of inland missions, roughly connecting St. Augustine and points west to the land of the Apalachee. Three of these missions were along the Suwannee, the second a little to the north of here and the third near present-day Luraville. The friars found that if the chiefs could be convinced to become Catholics, their people would, too. So the chiefs were converted by means of bribery, being given flour, tools, and blankets. Especially coveted were Spanish clothes. After a generation was converted to Catholicism, the next generation of Indians was raised as Catholic. But the generations kept becoming smaller as the natives fell victim to European diseases, to which they had little resistance. The interior missions eventually fell into disuse from lack of potential converts.

An alluring sandbar offered appealing views of the rivers' confluence. I wondered about the Indian and Spanish canoes that must have landed there. But it was off limits now, according to the "No Trespassing" sign. Sometimes the sheer number of "No Trespassing," "Keep Out," and "Private Property" signs made me wonder if a bunch of hooligans were hanging around the river. Property owners have rights I respect, but perhaps there were people who ignored those rights. The signs were a reflection of the times: less trust in our fellow citizens.

The limestone banks had pretty much given out below Branford, though there were limestone outcrops now and then. On higher ground were live oaks and pine. Low-slung humps of willow, river birch, and cypress lined the river. Behind many of these humps were extensive swamps that filled when summer's thunderstorms drifted over the Suwannee River Valley. Swamps are one of the most misunderstood and mischaracterized of Florida's ecosystems. Once considered vile places, full of mosquitoes, snakes, alligators, and other assorted evil creatures and suitable only for being drained, swamps are at last beginning to have their value recognized. At one time swamps covered more than half the state—tidal marshes near the coast, cedar swamps along rivers, still interior cypress swamps, open grassy bogs. Most swampland is inundated only part of the year. Yes, they can be buggy, but they serve the state well. Swamps provide a natural reservoir for runoff during floods. They fill up, then slowly percolate the water into the ground below, recharging the aquifer with clean, naturally filtered water, lessening runoff to the sea. Swamps are home to many creatures; their biodiversity is unmatched in other American wetlands. The lack of economic return works against preservation of wetlands. Private landowners do not have an incentive to preserve wetlands simply for the sake of doing good. Doing good doesn't pay the taxes on the land they own, or pay a dividend, so it doesn't support owners' families. Most American wetlands are privately owned.

The river widened further below the Santa Fe. It was now two hundred feet across, making a fairway for winds. But so far the winds hadn't been much of a problem. I paddled on, generally hugging one bank or the other, eventually coming to a spring near the hamlet of Wannamake. The waters of this spring were concreted in, with a wall between the river and the spring. Along the concrete was an elaborate deck. The owners had created their own private pool. I hope this spring damming wouldn't become a trend, though this was similar to bathhouses of an earlier era.

Quietly paddling over toward Turtle Springs, I startled a couple of turkeys—the big birds laboriously flapped their wings across the river. I wasn't sure they were going make it. There were some nice bass, small bream, and even smaller minnows darting among the shimmering grasses in the keyhole-shaped pool that fed a short run to the Suwannee. The depth of the water, the grasses, and the light of the day colluded to deliver every color combination of green and blue in the giant aquarium.

More houses showed up along the river. The increase in the size of the boats here corresponded to the increase in the breadth of the river. There also were—gasp!—jet skis, the bane of waters world-wide, in my opinion. I was thankful that they wouldn't be out at this time of year. Woe to the summertime paddler, drifting down-river in the morning mist, when a snowmobile of the water comes roaring around the bend. For starters, they are loud. Second, to have fun, the boaters drive around in circles, jumping their own wakes, like a dog chasing its tail. Get a couple together and they try to outdo each other, raising the stupidity and accident quotient exponentially. What can you do on a jet ski except speed? You can't fish. You can't travel overnight. The bigger ones, not really jet skis proper, can actually pull a conventional skier. As a hiker I have seen four-wheelers tear up and widen footpaths, and the jet ski is their cousin, except that it doesn't permanently tear up the water—just the ambiance.

Many signs alerted boaters to manatees in the area. I was getting closer to the Gulf. Manatees are not well adapted to sharing waters with motorized humanity on the Suwannee or any of Florida's rivers. Or perhaps I should say boaters have not adapted well to the manatee. In any case, the people are not going to go away, and manatees get the bad end of the deal. The crisis comes in the form of a propeller, sending a motorboat forward and taking a few manatees with it, as the big mammals feed on grasses in shallow waters. Around 90 percent of Florida's manatees have propeller scars on their backs indicating that they have survived a run-in with the whirling buzz saw.

Manatees first appeared on earth about 50 million years ago. The species in Florida waters is the West Indian manatee. In summer, they range from the coast of Mississippi all around the Florida shore and up the coast to Virginia, inhabiting rivers, canals, estuaries, and coastal areas. These mammals average an enormous ten to thirteen feet in length and weigh 800–1,200 pounds. They can live in fresh, salty, or brackish waters. In winter, when temperatures drop, they head for warmer waters, including springs on the Suwannee. Modern warm-water refuges include discharge areas of power plants on both coasts, allowing the animals to remain north of their historic wintering grounds. Manatees are found sporadically throughout the Caribbean. Other species occur in the Amazon River Basin, northeastern South America, and along the west coast of Africa.

Population estimates in Florida vary, but everyone agrees that the numbers are below four thousand animals. Manatees can live up to sixty years. A natural cause of their demise is cold weather. Human-related causes mainly involve collisions with boats, but manatees also get caught in currents from floodgates, are crushed in navigation locks, and are poached, vandalized, and accidentally entangled in fishing and crab trap lines. Habitat destruction is also stressing the population, so that all around, manatees are having a sufficiently hard time for it to be by no means clear that they will make another millennium. Not all is bad news, however. No Wake zones and increased public awareness of the manatee's plight may herald a reversal in these negative trends.

Creatures that seemed to be doing fine were the hawks. They were everywhere, perched on tree limbs, soaring over the woods—always looking majestic, classy, literally looking down on humanity and its ways. These were red-shouldered hawks, which prefer lowlands and swampy woods, both of course plentiful in Florida. They perch quietly, wait, then drop to catch insects, small mammals, snakes, and frogs. As noted, the alligator has made a comeback, and turtles were on every log.

Being above water, I didn't have much to worry about from motorboats. I paddled slowly and deliberately and came upon another spring. The next spring was not as apparent as others had been. Its spring run was much narrower than the spring itself, making it less obvious. I rolled the blade across the river. Rock Bluff Springs was on the left bank. Cypress trees with huge buttresses flanked the spring run. I paddled upstream toward a circular pool. Over the largest deep vent I dipped my water bottle into the spring water and took a big chug. Good. It didn't have that dissolved-organic-matter aftertaste like the main river did. These springs, just bubbling holes in the earth, were named for the conspicuous limestone bluff nearby, dotted with homes that scoffed at the floodwaters of the Suwannee, not built on pilings.

Beyond Rock Bluff, something furry caught my eye. Then its eye caught me: a beaver. At that instant, the beaver dove into the water. People often want wild animals to do something entertaining when spotted. What did I expect it to do—jump up on shore and sing and dance? Start furiously gnawing on a tree trunk? What they usually do is escape, as fast as possible, like the beaver did.

Dixie County. The South. I'm surprised there has not been a move to change the county name. I love the South and I love Dixie. I am very well traveled and wouldn't live anywhere else. Our southern history wasn't perfect and there's no denying it. But nor will I let the negative aspects of the past overwhelm the positive and unique cultural characteristics of this part of the country and bury them under political correctness. The state of Mississippi voted to keep the Confederate flag as part of its state flag. To me the Confederate flag represents southern pride and heritage, nothing more. For most, the flag has nothing to do with hate. You find me a pure symbol that hasn't been misused by some misguided group, and I will call you a good researcher. Satanists use crosses. Should we ban the cross? Should we ban the Confederate flag? Start banning symbols, and you are heading down a slippery slope that results in less freedom for everyone.

Dixie County had done well by Gornto Springs. The little county park had a small boat ramp, a few campsites, and a nice dock. It had a little development but not too much, unlike Hart Springs, on down the river in Gilchrist County, on the east side of the Suwannee. Gilchrist was the last county carved out of the state, coming to be on December 4, 1925. Hart Springs had a big campground, a camp store, a larger picnic area, even a ballfield, all this

Rock Bluff Springs was on the left bank. Cypress trees with huge buttresses flanked the spring run. I paddled upstream toward a circular pool.

spread far and wide around the spring boil, stripping away the natural feel of the site. It made the springs seem fake, as if piped in from somewhere and bubbling out of the ground like some bogus ride at, er, Orlando, giving people what they want—or what they think they want.

Around five in the afternoon I came to a low grassy bluff, partly shaded. On top stood a broken-down hunt shack, about ten by ten feet, on stilts. The mosquito screen on the window had peeled away, and I wasn't going to walk up the rickety stairs that led down to the river. Behind the shack I spied a magnificent live oak spreading wide from the river, a fine spot for a camp. The hard part was getting my gear from a tiny, sandy riverside beach up onto the bluff. A tangle of brush grew along the water. I struggled through the brambles, using cypress knees for secure footing. Up and down, bashing through the brush. As usual I went ahead and hauled everything from the boat, knowing that a nighttime gear run would be more of a hassle than just getting all of it at once. The daylight waned, reddened, and faded to gray. The mosquitoes didn't bother me that night—I must have lost a pint of blood the night before and had been driven to slumbering in the tent.

A muggy dawn. I loaded the boat under a thick layer of clouds that acted like a greenhouse. The river was still, save for a slight current. Before long I was stroking the blade in the dark day and passed another railroad bridge. It was an old one, old enough to feature a swivel from paddlewheel days, like the disused bridge I'd seen earlier. The swivel part of this bridge was no longer in use, but the bridge itself was still carrying the boxes rolling on steel wheels over the water. Patches of cement among the old and new timbers helped stabilize the bridge. which had been reworked repeatedly.

Just downriver are the remains of the last steamboat to work the river, the *City of Hawkinsville*. Homeported at Branford, the 141-foot steamboat made regular runs to Cedar Key and back in the employ of the lumber industry. Then the railroad came to Old Town, using the bridge I had just passed. In May of 1922, the *City of Hawkinsville* was abandoned by its captain, ending up in the depths of the river it once ran.

In no time I reached Old Town, the start of the longest continuous populated stretch of river. The houses were low-rises, all on pilings here in the floodplain and the swamps beyond the riverbanks, swamps ready to absorb flood runoff. Many of the homeowners had built makeshift bulkhead walls of all descriptions. Mostly made of stone, concrete, or wood, these barriers separated their property from the river. Bulkheads inhibit the river's ability to disperse excess water naturally—in other words, to flood. When strings of houses all have bulkheading, the effect is multiplied, as was the case here. Floodwaters are forced downriver. And woe to the homeowners below Old Town.

The U.S. Highway 98 bridge was the last one between the Gulf and the canoe. Bridges, to paddlers, are points of passage, like mileposts, definitively marking how far you have traveled. They often have landings and boat ramps nearby. Just below this bridge was Fanning Springs. It had once been an elaborate private development but had undergone many changes and was now a state recreation area. What it had lost in development it had gained in signs. Lots of signs. On the signs were rules. Lots of rules. The unchecked sprawl of signs fouled the natural atmosphere the state was supposedly trying to preserve. Unfortunately, in public areas agencies have to cater to those visitors who are going to do stupid things. Signs go up to stop them; otherwise they would plead ignorance and probably sue the state for damages caused by their own thoughtlessness. Lawyers, liability insurance, cost-benefit studies, actuaries, and the whole money-on-paper shuffle system—sometimes I can't believe this is the apex of civilization, the best we can do after all this time. (Most of the time, however, I see the glass as half full.)

The town of Fanning Springs, named for the once pristine, now sign-laden springs, is a product of the Seminole Wars. It started out as Fort Fanning in 1836. The fort was later occupied by Confederate troops during the Civil War. From here, they successfully sank a ninety-foot Union gunboat with cannon fire near the mouth of the springs. Divers can still see the gunboat. Beyond Fanning Springs lies Andrews Wildlife Management Area. This four-thousand-acre parcel, including the largest remaining tract of hardwood forest in the Suwannee Valley, was acquired in 1985 through the Save Our Rivers program. Though the old growth cypress was logged in the early 1900s, four Florida State Champion trees remain: Florida maple, persimmon, river birch, and bluff oak. Oaks, cedars, birches, and palms graced the low limestone bluff. From this point, with a couple of exceptions, the east bank was wild all the way to and including Manatee Springs State Park. The banks lowered further. Cattails and sawgrass appeared. In some places, the shoreline was indefinite—just a ragged row of cypress trees along the water, with a seemingly infinite swamp beyond.

Save Our Rivers is the pretty name for the Florida Water Management Lands Trust Fund. Created by the state legislature, this fund gets its money from the state documentary taxes and Preservation 2000, a fund earmarked for land purchase. Land is bought only on a willing-seller basis. It is then restored to natural conditions except for river access points, nature trails, and posting of boundary lines. Since the trust fund was established, the Suwannee River Water Management District, which covers fifteen counties, has acquired forty-seven thousand acres along the Suwannee, including 70 percent of the river frontage in the upper basin.

The paddle up Manatee Springs Run was the climax of the seventeen-mile day. The clear waters shaded by tall cypress were much more appealing than the more developed Hart Springs. An otter popped its head out of the water and greeted me before my landing: welcome to Manatee Springs. I had stayed here before and looked forward to reaching the camp. Manatee Springs has a quality campground and was an easy inclusion in my book *Best in Tent Camping: Florida*. I walked around and found a ranger, Karen Luzader, who politely took me to the entrance station to pay for a campsite. The ride was much appreciated—it would have been a hot, boring road walk to the hut. It turned out that Karen had lived around the area for years, working at Hart Springs, of all places, before landing a job here. I appreciated her help as she hauled my gear in her truck to my campsite. It was time to start organizing for the transition from canoe to sea kayak. I was due for some serious paring down of gear.

The great naturalist William Bartram lauded the natural beauty of this area, and when Florida began planning for state parks, Manatee Springs was one of the first places that came to mind. The combination of the historic Suwannee River, a huge spring, varied plant communities, and a mammal reserve made Manatee Springs an easy choice. The spring itself is impressive. It boils up over eighty thousand gallons of clear water per minute. A viewing path lies all around the springhead, where you can look into the water and see lots of fish, turtles, and other aquatic life. Just below the spring's beginning is a roped-off swimming area. A calmer pool area has been built across the spring and is accessible by a short foot trail. Viewing platforms have been erected for peering out into the water to look for manatees. At the end of the board-walk is a dock for boaters, anglers, and manatee watchers.

Before enjoying the park's attributes, I set up camp. At the next campsite over were some friendly RV campers named Bob and Cheryl. When he retired after thirty years in the navy, they had sold their home and had been living out of their camper for a year—and planned on doing so for the rest of their days. They were loving life. Bob had once been stationed in Key West and they were going down to see the changes that had taken place in the last twenty-five years. I was sure the changes at Key West would overwhelm them. They took pity on their paddler neighbor and fed me dinner—a Cajun recipe they had gotten in New Orleans—while they entertained me with tales of a full-time life on the road. Their theme was adventure, seeing the unseen, and meeting folks who never would have walked down the street past their old home.

During the night dew gathered on the branches of the pines, live oaks, and palms, gaining momentum, dragged by gravity and dripping off the leaves, landing drop by drop with quiet thuds on

the ground. The cool of the morning was just passing as light infil-
trated the eastern sky. Soon, the sun would burn across the clear
winter skies.

Later that morning Bob pulled his truck around and hauled me
and my gear down to the canoe launch. The help was appreciated.
Bob wished me luck. I was off down Manatee Springs Run, initially at the swiftest pace I would travel all day. Then the river
turned southwest into a wicked headwind, averaging about fifteen
miles per hour with gusts up to thirty-five, the radio said. It sure
felt like it. I worked the canoe as close to the bank as I could to
minimize the wind, now and then crossing the wide river to get to
the calmer side. It was slow going, somewhat like the efforts at
rebuilding Gulf sturgeon populations on the Suwannee River. I
imagined there to be a sturgeon under me at that moment, though
it was a little early in the season for them to be here. The Gulf
sturgeon is an ancient fish that first appeared on earth 225 million
years ago. Now ranging from Florida to Louisiana, it spends time
in the Gulf and in rivers like the Suwannee. The long, spring-fed
Suwannee represents its best inland habitat. On hot summer days
sturgeon cool off just downstream of spring flows, staying in the
river between March and November. They can grow up to ten feet
long, weigh up to twelve hundred pounds, and live forty years.
Their toothless mouths work like a vacuum, sucking up mollusks,
crabs, worms, and shrimp. Gulf sturgeon are listed as threatened
under the Endangered Species Act.

The weather was changing. A front was moving in, that much
was obvious. Near Yellow Jacket Landing, on the far bank, I felt as
if I were in a still life painting, despite continuous paddling. The
headwind was winning. Cattails swayed back and forth then returned to their original positions, laughing at the wind and at me.
Stretching from this point along the north bank was the Lower
Suwannee National Wildlife Refuge—pristine riverside scenery
off-limits to houses and development but also off-limits to camp-

ing. The refuge protects a large section of the lower Suwannee River basin and also fronts twenty-six miles of the Gulf Coast, making this one of the largest undeveloped river deltas in the United States. The area includes habitats ranging from tidal marshes to pine woods on higher ground. This is just one of more than 520 refuges in the national wildlife refuge system covering 93 million acres in our country.

The wind whipped up further. There were bona fide whitecaps on the river, banging the bow of the boat and making it hard to keep straight. I finally called it quits near Fowler's Bluff, a narrow stretch of land high enough to support a few pine trees and a few houses with people living in them—everywhere else was cypress swamp. I did the usual unloading and setting up of camp. This camp offered a special surprise: the trip's first batch of no-see-ums. I'd forgotten the misery these little bugs, more like teeth with wings, can dish out. Soon I changed into long pants, a long-sleeved shirt, socks, and hat, even though the temperature was in the upper 70s. Any exposed skin was covered with bug dope.

At dusk, bats flitted in black silhouettes from the open sky over the water into the trees, wheeling and dipping in flight. It was easy to see how they had become objects of mystery and derision. For starters, they are the only mammals that can fly—right there they are distinguished from all other flying creatures. They only come out at night, fly in odd patterns, and hang upside down, their strange ways giving rise to such myths as their being the animal incarnation of vampires. Bats can flap their wings—really long fingers interconnected by skinlike membranes—six to eight times per second. These nocturnal creatures have decent eyesight, but it is their well-known sonar capability known as echolocation that helps them get around and catch prey in the dark. Bats emit high frequency calls, inaudible to humans, that bounce off objects so that the return signals are detected by their oversized ears.

Florida's northern yellow bat, Seminole bat, and evening bat are insect eaters, chasing individual bugs through the air or in trees. Sometimes they swoop open-mouthed through swarms of insects, getting their fill. They are less active in winter, when insects are fewer. I hoped the bats were taking out a few no-see-ums.

Some other creatures in the war on biting insects are dragonflies and water striders. Dragonflies are aptly named and all but breathe fire, specializing in mosquito extermination. After 300 million years of evolution, they are pretty efficient, too. Their legs are attached just behind the head, which keeps them from walking but allows them to grasp prey and tear it apart with their jaws. Don't be surprised when some "insect rights" group tries to change the DNA of dragonflies so they consume their prey in a much more "humane" fashion than tearing them limb from limb while still alive. Their four powerful wings each move independently, allowing dragonflies to fly forward, backward, up, and down. There are around 150 varieties in the state. Water striders are those long-legged bugs that walk on water, also known as Jesus-bugs. They feed in fresh water on mosquito larvae, getting the swamp angels before they turn into flying bloodsuckers.

I sat outside the tent, leaning against a tree trunk, as the campfire flickered. Nighttime was always the time of reflection on the day and on what lay ahead. Of immediate concern was the lightning flashing in northwest sky. It put on a show for a good four hours before rain finally peppered the tent. I wasn't worried about getting wet; the Eureka Timberline had served me well and would again. The front was here; I retired to my reliable refuge. Lightning is a predictable part of the Florida skyscape. The state has the most "thunderstorm days" in the continental United States, seventy to ninety days per year; as defined by the National Weather Service, these are days when lightning strikes within a fifteen-mile radius of a weather station. Generally speaking, a lightning flash can't be seen beyond fifteen miles away. This lightning was certainly within the scope of my camp. Throughout the night thunder rumbled and sheets of rain swept across the Suwannee River, hitting my tent like bursts of machine-gun fire. Winds whipped through the woods, blowing trees to the point of breaking. I awoke off and on, wondering what it was going to be like on the river when daylight came. Finally, nerves got the better of me and I got up for good at 5:30 A.M. to see what monsters I was about to face. The winds were sure to be higher in the afternoon than they were now. The loading process offered another surprise—a tidal change in the river, the first of the trip. The sea was near. It was ten minutes to seven, mostly dark, when I set out on the river. I followed the outgoing tide, paddling as hard as possible. In rapid succession I passed Fowlers Bluff, the last community on the river, then Little Turkey Island, the refuge visitor center, and Turkey Island proper.

The Suwannee was all wild past Fowlers Bluff. The counties bordering the Gulf here have always been some of the state's wildest and least populous. High, dry islands encircled by impenetrable swamps leading to coastal marshes made for good hiding places for deserters during the Civil War. Sometimes these runaways acted independently, hiding out alone. Others grouped together, forming semi-military bands for mutual protection. One group, just north of the Suwannee, was known as the Independent Rangers of Taylor County. Confederate deserters, they drew up a constitution swearing allegiance to the United States and had all the men sign it. A provision of this constitution was punishment by death for deserting the group. What irony—deserters banding together, with death resulting for any deserter from a group of deserters. Occasionally, the Confederate army swept through in search of the deserters, using dogs and burning down dwellings. One raid in the valley of the Econfina River was so effective that the men offered to come in on their own and raise cattle for the Rebels in lieu of carrying rifles. The Grays rejected this offer and continued the roundup, but 1864 records indicate only 220 deserters restored to the ranks.

The winds shifted to the northwest, which left most of the river protected for a while. That is, until I got near East Pass, where the river turned northwest and I pushed headlong into the wind with no cover. Dead into the wind, the last mile to the hamlet of Suwannee was pure hell. The winds were easily twenty-five miles per hour. I was hugging the bank, hoping for some break from the wind, paddling through brackish water inches deep, punching into mud and pushing forward, getting blown back after every stroke. The wind roared in my ears as my arms strained to keep the canoe straight. Eventually I made Demory Creek and Jane Connor's house, where my sea kayak was stored. The whole scene seemed surreal when the canoe hit the sandy beach by her house. I couldn't quite believe I had just paddled 230 miles down the Suwannee River. It seemed to have happened so fast, yet the last mile was so defeatingly slow. I also couldn't quite believe that I was about to reload the gear and jump into a sea kayak to paddle on to the Keys. Even with the weather as foul as it was, I knew it was time to go. My visualization of this moment had been a far cry from the reality. In my imagined picture I was wearing short pants and a T-shirt, and a gentle breeze lapped waves against the shoreline. I would casually change boats, listening to gulls squawk in the distance. But it was not to be.

The temperature had dropped into the 40s. Gusty bursts of wind cut through the layers of clothing on my body. I immediately set about paring down my gear, as the sea kayak would handle much less weight than the canoe. This boat was a brand new Old Town Millennium, later proven to be exceptional in the Gulf. Jane came out to greet me and invited me in for a cup of coffee. Her hospitality and house warmed me up. I gave her a brief overview of

The winds shifted to the northwest, which left most of the river protected for a while.

the adventure so far, then she helped me put the canoe under a shed near the house.

It was time to wedge food and gear into the sea kayak. I could fit some food into the compartments, but then the stove and cook kit wouldn't fit. My tent would fit, but my books and charts wouldn't. Something was going to have to stay in Jane's shed. Once inside the shed, I would find something that might be needed for the journey, like an extra cooking pot, and return it to the kayak. I went back and forth, bringing a little gear to the kayak, returning a little more to the shed. Finally, by late afternoon, the kayak was finally loaded. With a little trepidation I paddled into the Suwannee River but just a very short distance—a dry run, you might say—over to Miller's Marina, where there was a campground. Later Jane dropped by a couple of supply items I had asked her to grab.

An Australian, Jane is comfortable around boats. She is a sailor and a fellow writer. She and her husband had moved from California to Suwannee because it was a place where they could keep their sailboat in the water and actually afford a home on water. California prices for that are out of sight for most. I had contacted Jane through the town of Suwannee's chamber of commerce, which had given me her telephone number. She was immediately receptive to my request, although I was a complete stranger. I gave her references to check; whether she checked them I don't know. But before setting off from Griffis Camp in Georgia, I had driven the sea kayak down here, met Jane, and stored the boat and supplies in her shed. Trust is refreshing and restores one's sometimes shaken faith in humanity.

Miller's Marina Campground was an RV enclave. Being a tent camper, I stuck out like a mobile home in Beverly Hills. But I wasn't concerned—night was falling and I wanted to get a shower before it grew any colder. It was chilly stripping off in the shower room. I danced under the nozzle until the water warmed me. Afterwards, I shook off like a dog, drip drying as long as possible before dressing, still a little on the damp side. A towel had failed to make the cut back at home. I returned to the wind-blown mesh shelter and sought out some grub. Darkness didn't exactly swallow Miller's Marina, with lights twinkling from some of the RVs, but it was dark and quiet enough to mull over the mixed qualities of the day. The hot shower had felt good; even the most seasoned adventurer appreciates one now and then. I had completed a successful run all the way down to the delta of the Suwannee River. Triumph! The relaxation of a celebratory cup of coffee in an actual living room had yielded to busy details of gear selection for transfer to the sea kayak. And the stiff wind and hard paddling on the wide estuary probably served as clues to what lay ahead.

Part 11

THE

5 The Nature Coast

The stove had to melt a little ice in the pot the next morning before the water was warm enough for my morning coffee. The morning sun melted the frost off the kayak as I made another trial-and-error loading. To explain loading the sea kayak requires explaining the boat itself. Sea kayaks come in a series of shapes and sizes. My Old Town Millennium was known as a touring kayak. It was 17 feet, 4 inches long, 22.5 inches wide, and 13 inches deep and weighed 60 pounds. Its load-carrying capacity, including one human being, was 325 pounds. A sea kayak is a slim, low, enclosed boat. It is decked on top and pointed at both bow and stern. A hole, the cockpit, lies in the center of the boat. This is where the paddler sits, sliding into the boat feet first. The cockpit of this boat was 17 by 34 inches. The paddler's legs are stretched forward and parallel with the water. The kayaker's seat has a back for support and there are braces in which to place your feet. Since the boat and the paddler are so close to the water, kayakers must wear what is known as a "spray skirt" while paddling. This skirt made of neoprene is donned by pulling it over your head and then positioning it around your waist, tightly enough to resist water entry. The outer part of the spray skirt is hooked onto the rim of the cockpit to prevent water from splashing inside, keeping the paddler dry and the kayak above water.

The deck of the kayak has two watertight hatches. It is into these hatches that the paddler's gear goes. Loading gear into the compartments through the small hatches required planning. These compartments have much less room than there is in a canoe, but that is the price for being able to track better and generally go faster than in a canoe. Each hatch is covered with a neoprene seal then cinched down via straps with a plastic hatch cover. Smart kayakers store their gear according to their needs, trying to avoid having to open and close the hatches repeatedly to get at things, which can't be done by the paddler without getting out of the boat. More storage space lies on the kayak's deck. Elastic cords allow gear to be stored atop the deck. However, this gear must be secured in watertight dry bags to withstand water splashing over the deck. I kept a small dry bag attached to the boat immediately at hand for items such as sunglasses, bug dope, sunscreen, etc. Additional storage space is in the cockpit. This was where I kept the day's water, lunch, and snacks. A small carrying handle was attached to each end of the boat. Onto the handle I tied ropes for docking, pulling the boat, and securing items on the boat deck.

Although water splashes more easily onto a kayak, this boat is safer in open water than a canoe. Being enclosed, it is less liable to fill with water and sink. My touring kayak was much narrower and more tippy than a canoe, yet it tracked straighter and faster in the water. Of course, this shape also made the boat less maneuverable. Because it was long and narrow, it was more difficult to turn on a dime. A kayak is powered by a single paddle with blades on both ends. This way the paddler gets more effective strokes per minute and doesn't have to switch sides to dip the blade. Part of the steer-

To explain loading the sea kayak requires explaining the boat itself. My Old Town Millennium was known as a touring kayak. It was 17 feet, 4 inches long, 22.5 inches wide, and 13 inches deep and weighed 60 pounds.

ing is done with the paddle. Kayaks have another steering mechanism—the rudder. Not all kayaks have rudders, but most touring kayaks do. This rudder, about a foot long, could be pulled in and out of the water via a cord on pulleys accessible to the paddler while in the cockpit. The rudder is steered by the foot braces, also known as pedals, inside the kayak. Pushing the right or left pedal would turn the rudder. It takes time for paddlers to learn the steering intricacies of using two foot pedals and a double-bladed paddle, in addition to other things like body lean, wind, tides, and waves. Eventually, you steer the boat without thinking about it, much like driving a car that has a clutch and stick shift.

Overall, a sea kayak was the best choice for the big water, especially considering winds that were likely to blow in the Gulf. Because of its low profile, a kayak is less affected by winds than is a much taller, broad-sided canoe. Comfortwise, a sea kayak isn't even in the same league as a canoe, no matter who makes it. The color of the boat, which I did not name (nor did I name the canoe), was off-white; Old Town calls it granite. The boat was made of Polylink 3, a three-layer plastic, designed to be stiff yet light and to provide insulation from cold and noise. It worked fine. I had been an Old Town man for many years, using their canoes, and when the time came to get a sea kayak, I naturally turned to them. They had been in the boat business for over a century.

Their story starts in 1898, in Old Town, Maine, on the banks of the Penobscot River. George Gray and A. E. Wickett began building canoes behind Gray's hardwood store. By 1914 they had become the world's largest canoe manufacturers, operating out of a big red-brick building still in use today. They began making kayaks in 1940. The old models were of wood and canvas. Old Town had their own lumber harvesting operation, using horses, until 1956. Like all other manufacturers, they later began making plastic boats, which are overwhelmingly popular now. The city of Old Town calls itself "Canoe City."

Sea kayaks themselves are much older than is Old Town. Their design is generally attributed to northern natives of the Arctic, from the Bering Strait to Baffin Island. Their boats were built using wood frames lashed together with animal sinew and covered in sealskin. Each shape and design was as individual as the individual builder, though general patterns developed. Florida's seagoing Indians generally used dugout canoes, very long, built of hollowed-out cypress trunks.

The short trial run with the sea kayak was a good idea. The boat was new to me, and getting used to this model took a little time, though I had paddled many other kayaks previously. I had never gotten into this kayak until I loaded it at Jane's for the first time the day before. I had had the canoe and sea kayak shipped to the business of Bob Phillips (Chris's dad) in Jacksonville and thus hadn't tried them until it was actually time to put them to use.

I needed a few things back at Jane's house, so I paddled back that way. The low tide in Demory Creek forced me to pull the sea kayak up into mud below the beach in front of the house. A ten-foot-wide rampart of muck lay between dry land and me. I wasn't going to wait for the tide to rise, so I debarked. At the first bare-footed step I sank ankle deep into stinky black muck, but I plunged ahead to reach the beach, wanting to grab a few extra clothes and my forgotten spoon from the shed. This was my camping spoon that always goes out with me. I got it a few years back. It has a fat blue handle and a small lip. I like it because I associate it with adventuring in the backcountry, whether it be by land or sea.

Jane bid me farewell from the porch, getting a little laugh out of my muddiness. She rustled up a long board that I used to bridge the muck between the sand and water to get back to the boat. The board helped but didn't quite reach all the way. Getting into the boat was an interesting proposition. As soon as I placed one foot inside the kayak, the boat broke free of the mud and began to drift out into the water. As my legs were pulled apart, I quickly pushed away from the board with my landward foot and threw myself backward into the boat, landing hard but keeping my muck-laden feet from soiling the inside of the new craft. I slid the boat out a little and washed the mud off my feet with seawater, cold notwithstanding. I was sick of working around the cold. The cold wasn't going to kill me, and I needed to toughen up. When winter backpacking, I was always mentally ready for cold. Here in Florida, I had been ready for more warmth than had presented itself; though I knew full well that cold happens here.

Thus my departure from Jane's house was rather less classy and memorable than I had imagined it would be. All glamour was lost here. I mentally listed excuses for my amateur actions: I was getting used to the new craft, and the cold, windy conditions weren't favorable for experimentation. Pity; but the boat and I would know each other well enough by the time we reached the Keys.

Ahead were the river mouth and the Gulf. I stroked the new paddle, enjoying the efficiency of the double blades, and set out for East Pass, a southward channel at the mouth of the Suwannee. Did the double blades mean I would be making 4,000 strokes per day? The stroke motions were completely different. In the canoe, with the single-bladed canoe paddle, you stroke the blade on one side of the boat or the other. With the sea kayak paddle, you alternately dip the blade in on either side of the boat, with arms more or less forward of you. Repeat enough of either and you'll get somewhere, though sea kayaking is undoubtedly more efficient, given equal conditions. Repeat enough of either and your arms will feel like mincemeat.

I paddled into sunlight pouring off the water where wind tore the surface into a million diamonds of light, entering the East Pass channel. The farther down I went, the brinier it grew. Cypress groves gave way to saltmarsh grass. The horizon opened to offer an immense sky. Wispy clouds drifted in the distance. After a few twists and turns, East Pass widened. I rounded a bend and there it was—the Gulf of Mexico! The tide was now coming in, pushing the boat back, so I just sat there and reveled in the wonderment of having paddled the Suwannee River all the way to salt water. The Gulf was a waypoint of note. The moment passed and I paddled southward—the ocean extended to the limit of vision, keeping the deeps to the west and the marshes eastward, scattered and broken by palm hammocks and cypress domes far in the distance. Fishing boats were just specks on the watery horizon. The Gulf was impossibly open, especially compared to the narrow upper Suwannee. Seagrass waved in the transparent aqua. I was pumped up and ready to paddle south.

Up to this point I had had a Florida gazetteer to help me roughly keep up with where I was on the Suwannee River. From here on I was using nautical charts. These coastal maps indicate channels, buoys, land, water depths, and more. The charts greatly aided my decision making and knowing exactly where I was, which was easier moment to moment than while on the Suwannee. In one sense I could have done without them—all I needed to do was head south along the coast, keeping the land to my left. But on the other hand, half the fun was in navigating. I do mean half, because soon my adventures in navigating would alter the trip. Yes, I could have brought a Global Positioning System (GPS) unit to tell me where I was all the time. But in that case, why not simply get a motorboat and ride, or let someone else do the driving? Navigating, self-propelled travel, weather, strangers, and not knowing what was coming next were ingredients that add up to adventure.

The chart was folded into a clear plastic map holder and strapped to elastic boat cords with Velcro. The chart indicated the island ahead to be Deer Island. The green belt above the ocean slowly evolved into individual trees with stretches of beach. A good boat landing in a cove overlooked the Gulf. A rising tide enabled me to bring the boat close to the beach. Rich woodland of live oak, cedar, palms, and pine grew just beyond the shore. After debarking, I pulled the boat up and stood there taking in the scene—on a shell-laden island beach, overlooking the Gulf, blasts of wind pushing the salty water against the narrow island, waves crashing at my feet, all under that famous Florida sun. A motorboat landed as I stood there taking it all in. Two guys jumped from the craft. One of them walked into the water, fishing the cove while the other guy walked my way. We met on the beach and began to talk. They turned out to be two outdoor veterans who had explored much of the Nature Coast, as this area was known. They were in their mid-forties and had been here before. The two of us walked to the interior of the island and spied a fantastic campsite out of the wind, yet with a decent view of the Gulf. The two fishing buddies had had a poker tournament at this very site many years before. Was this history? Was this Florida history? What makes history? Is it what Indians did way back when, or a few guys having a poker tournament out on an uninhabited island? History is very subjective. Ask two people who have just witnessed an auto wreck.

The motorboaters had seen changes in Florida and truly appreciated the immense diversity of the state's wildscapes. The Nature Coast stood a chance. Ranging from Wakulla County south of Tallahassee to northern Pasco County, just north of Tampa, the Nature Coast already has nearly a million acres under public domain, among them Crystal River National Wildlife Refuge and Apalachicola National Forest. Paper companies hold other vast tracts. But what it really has going for it, conservation-wise, is a scarcity of beaches. Marsh, woods, and mangrove form the coast. This has kept the hotel-beach-all-you-can-eat-buffet syndrome at bay. The waters of the Nature Coast are generally shallow and not big-boat friendly. Visitors to this undeveloped area come to realize that the wildlife and natural beauty are better than a beach of imported sand, backed by high-rise hotels and flanked by fast food joints. Not only is the beauty easy on the eye, but it draws in environmentally conscious tourists who tend to go easy on the land.

The beachcomber and I agreed that a balance of conservation and development was needed on the Nature Coast. He gave me a gallon of water, in two half-gallon jugs. I had only containers enough for two crucial gallons, a forgotten detail back at Jane's. Pretty stupid to forget something as important on a sea kayaking trip as containers for fresh water. After setting up camp, I toured Deer Island. Laughing gulls were grouped at the water's sandy edge. A conglomeration of shells formed the northwest end of the island, probably an old Indian midden. A midden, in essence, is a trash pile. Indians gathered shellfish from the ocean and discarded the uneaten portions, along with other trash from their lives, and piled them up, evidence that Deer Island was a shellfish bonanza for the hungry ancients. Archeologists consider middens a window on the lives of those who left them. Scientists are already digging through modern garbage, too, for what it reveals about our lives.

I swung around to the east side of the island—mostly marsh with a few red mangrove trees. This is the northerly limit of this coastal tree. Mangroves are among the few kinds of trees that can tolerate growing in salt water. The secret for them is the ability to process the salt water by secreting excess salt through their leaves.

The red mangrove is also known as the "walking tree." This tree grows at the water's edge, its trunk supported by numerous tangled red roots, known as prop roots, since they prop up the trunk of the tree. These roots give the tree its nickname—it seems to walk on water. Mangroves benefit Florida's coastline in multiple ways. They provide a sort of protective nursery for small fish, crustaceans, and shellfish, which in turn are fed on by larger fish. Mangroves are rookery sites for coastal birds, like pelicans and roseate spoonbills. Human coastal residents get the benefit of mangroves absorbing wind and waves coming inland, stabilizing shorelines with their roots.

Mangroves reproduce in an interesting way. Seeds sprout on the tree, and a miniature live mangrove eventually drops down into the water. From there the winds, currents, and tides find it a home, where it roots and grows to produce offshoots of its own. Thus you might say it's a walking tree in habit as well as in appearance. The tropical mangroves here were small. The Suwannee area is the mangrove equivalent of the North Pole, the most northerly latitude where mangroves survive; cold snaps like the one I'd paddled through can kill them. They fare much better in South Florida, especially in the Everglades, where they reach their greatest heights and concentrations.

From the mangroves, I banged and bashed my way to the island interior, where a small evergreen shrub, yaupon, grew abundantly. Florida's Indians made a concoction from yaupon berries that English speakers called "black drink." The berries of yaupon make an emetic, and the Indians drank the black drink and threw up, purging themselves during certain rituals. That's the funny thing about Indian words: we often cannot know exactly what they were, what they meant, or how they sounded—we only know the English corruptions. Florida Indians may have called the drink "eye of the god," for all we know.

The appropriately named Spanish bayonet, a bush with sharp pointed leaves, ambushed my legs at every opportunity as I walked through the dense growth. I found a couple of other camps, flagged by beer cans. Stacks of crab traps were piled by an old tin-roofed shack. In the marshy edge a bird, an American bittern, waded the shallows, slowly and methodically searching for an aquatic meal. It spotted me and froze with its bill pointing skyward, trying to blend in with the background of marsh grasses. One of the most fascinating aspects of God's creatures is the individuality of the evolutionary tracks whereby creatures thrive and reproduce. The bittern's implausible defense has worked well enough for it to be embedded in the genetic program.

The wind picked up and I retired to my selected campsite. I lay down in the warm sun on a three-inch-thick bed of pine needles, smoking a big old cigar and doing some thinking. How unfortunate that natural beauty sometimes provokes its own demise, by way of human mess-making. For if a natural creation is never viewed, how can its beauty be gauged? To be gauged, it must be seen. Once seen, it gains attention. But gaining human attention may bring its downfall and possible demise. My life seemed so short and insignificant when compared with God's creations. What lasting contributions would or could or should I make on this earth? To this earth? *Or was my function as a human being to tread lightly, then go away?* What was my purpose? What was the purpose of this land? This journey was just one foray among many, all amounting to a lifetime spent trying to answer such questions.

Later, I enjoyed my first Gulf sunset of the year. The colors imperceptibly yet unmistakably transformed from yellow to red to orange to pink to gray. I sat before the fire—the temperature had already dipped into the 40s—turning back every once in a while to see the sky darkening through the intertwined limbs of live oaks. The wind died and the night quieted, save for the hissing of firewood, as the fallen tide and lack of wind rendered the ocean mute. The sounds of the woods, especially my hoot owl companions on the Suwannee, were conspicuously absent as I drifted to sleep under the stars by the fire, feeling the soreness of a new way of paddling. This workout was better than I could get in any health club. In the days of the Indians and settlers, just getting along from day to day required plenty of hard work and exercise for the average person. Nowadays, most modern people hunt only money, instead of directly seeking food and shelter. Most jobs consist of button pushing, talking on the phone, watching something. A few hundred years ago the thinking world would have laughed at people pedaling away on stationary bikes, lifting weights, and doing calisthenics by the name of aerobics, led by a personal trainer. You'd think with all the mirrors in those fancy health clubs that some of those spinners would notice they were going nowhere fast.

The cold night dipped below freezing again. Once I got up, I noticed that the tide was low, way low. A big mud flat separated me from the water, so I waited for it to come to me. I hung around the campfire, drinking coffee and warming my toes—through three pairs of socks. Remember, wood warms you three times: when you gather it, when you break it up, and when you burn it. Sometimes it'll do a little more, besides—like burn things held too close to burning wood. My wool socks were burning with my feet inside! I pulled my dogs away, but the damage was done. The outer pair was ruined. The remainder of said socks went into the fire, stinking up the camp with an odor much like that of human hair burning.

I was now anxious to leave Deer Island, one pair of socks short. With the wind sure to put up a fight soon, I struck out across the muck to the water. Tow rope in hand, I set forth, bare feet dipping into the mud. Every step made a sucking sound, *glop, glop, glop*, as my foot emerged from the cold and salty slop. The kayak slid easily enough across the flat, which had just enough sand to keep me from going too deep. I left the boat at the edge of the water and returned for a gear run. Carrying 50 pounds of gear in addition to my 185 pounds, I sank deeper into the muck. The load also made balancing trickier, but I eventually got my gear and myself water-borne without any major mishaps. Finally, the boat was ready go and I dropped into the cockpit with my legs splayed, washing my feet off again. This sea muck comes off a body about as easily as super glue. The water seemed warmer than the air, and it probably was, since the air temperature was hovering just a touch above freezing.

The tide slowly came in, and I decided to cut through the Raleigh Islands, some clumps of marsh, toward the mainland. More land offered more navigational challenges and opportunities as well as varying the paddle. I made the mistake of grounding myself, despite the incoming tide. There just wasn't enough water to float the boat. I backtracked and paddled far from land around the Long Cabbage Islands, trying to get a little depth. The water deepened beyond Derrick Key Gap, a deep spot where boats could cut though the shallows and isles. Beyond the gap I obstinately gambled on a shortcut back inland, through some oyster bars and low marsh islands, to reach the north side of Cedar Key. Here, I decided to cut between Cedar Key and the mainland. I was soon passing by Goose Creek without problems and patting myself on the back for being so smart and efficient. The bridge connecting the mainland and Cedar Key was visible ahead. Once under the bridge I'd stop somewhere to get water and keep east into big Waccasassa Bay, which lay beyond Cedar Key. Although the tide was still rising, the oyster bars outnumbered those on the charts and choked the waterway. I finally went under the bridge.

It was now a little past noon. The wind was picking up. I turned southerly, trying to find a marina with some drinking water. Ahead of me lay a maze of oyster bars and marsh grasses. It was hard to find a bead on a good route from water level in a sea kayak. Tides vary, and it was evident that this high tide was not going to be that high. Indeed it proved to be a very low high tide, never covering much of the oyster bars.

I pushed on against my better judgment, firmly deciding to test my navigational prowess. After all, I had written *A Paddler's Guide to Everglades National Park*, which I knew well. But having written a paddling guidebook doesn't make a tide rise high enough to paddle among oyster bars. I should have realized that the tide was not going to rise high enough for me to cut between Cedar Key and the mainland. Ahead was a shallow channel with about two inches of water, then nothing but mud beyond. I flipped the rudder up, trying to continue through the channel, then shortly grounded the boat. I would have to backtrack out of the dead end. I began to back up into the wind, slowly pushing the paddle into the mud, moving just a few feet at a time. When the water became deep enough I would flail with the paddle—half in the water, half in the mud, splattering myself as the wind kicked gray-brown muck all over me. Just an inch less depth would stop me again. This was beginning to be a nightmare. The mud was so deep that getting out and walking the boat out was not an option. Using all the force I could muster, I kept paddling backward, rowing you might say, and actually made a little headway.

With this encouraging development, I tried to turn the boat around and paddle forward. But as I swung the boat around, the wind stopped me from making the U turn and blew me back into the cove, back into the mud where I had started. The bridge to Cedar Key was within sight, and I was putting on a free show for the incoming tourists. This was getting embarrassing and frustrating. I channeled my embarrassment and powered the Old Town from the mud. The boat was pointed stern to the wind. I began pushing/paddling the boat backward, somehow reaching deeper water. I quickly flipped the rudder back down, made the complete turn into the wind, and tiredly paddled back to the bridge, mud covered and daunted. This episode once again proved that most shortcuts don't work, especially in the outdoors.

I stopped for a minute at a landing beside the bridge. A fellow in a small rubber boat with a little motor was putting in, to go out to a larger motorboat he had grounded the day before. I asked him about a marina and he said there was one at the next bridge south. I bid him good luck with troubles I understood all too well. The wind blew strongly and I paddled west into it. The deeper water was a double-edged sword. Depth made the paddling easier, yet it also made the waves bigger. But at least I *could move*. I wrangled my way south among more oyster bars and somehow came within sight of the second bridge. A dock lay just ahead—except it wasn't the alleged marina but a shellfish processing plant. Nature Coast Industries. I docked anyway—my arms were jiggly from all the fruitless paddling back in the cove. I pulled up the Old Town and walked to the parking lot where three men stood together, smoking and talking. Being a guy, I normally hate asking for directions, especially from hardened locals. It's even worse when you ask for directions while splattered in ocean muck and wearing a plastic spray skirt. At this point, however, I was too tired, too wet, and too cold to care. I asked a few questions about somewhere to camp on Cedar Key, and they directed me to a campground about a quarter mile up the road. Wild and rustic sites were not to be had on this island. The clammers let me leave the boat there while I hauled my gear to the campground under the bright but weak sun, walking along the roadside, gear slung over my shoulder, feeling like a hobo. The clammers must have been laughing it up as I walked away. I would have been.

The camp keeper was inside the small and spartan office. A curtain separated the office from his living quarters, from which he emerged. Gil was his name. I asked about camping. "Look around and find a site," he said. Once again I was the only tent camper. Of the forty or fifty campsites, more than half were occupied full-time, so this wasn't your average campground. A fellow walking his sheep dog came by. Our eyes met and he said hello. I soon spilled out my story to Deford and how I had ended up on Cedar Key. It turned out that he hailed from Kentucky, near Lexington. He offered to take me down and get my boat—that way I could keep it with me safely. I took Deford up on the offer, and off we went in his big diesel-powered truck to retrieve the boat. The time came to pay Gil. Gil was about seventy, missing many teeth, and looked as if he had worked hard all his life. He still worked hard, keeping this campground in shape. Gil had lived all over Florida. "I was in Miami in the 1940s, you wouldn't recognize it. The traffic was lighter than in Gainesville today," he said. I went to take a shower, trying to imagine actually being able to get around Miami in a leisurely way rather than sitting at a dead stop on Dixie Highway near the University of Miami, sun beating through the car windows.

The screened-in bathhouse had no heat. (What did I expect, the Taj Mahal?) I stripped down and jumped in the shower. The soap was working its magic as the hot water ran out. I briefly considered leaving the soap on and saying to heck with the shower, but that would probably feel worse than being layered in saltwater scum. Instead, I did the shower nozzle shiver dance during the rinse cycle. Quickly donning my not-too-clean clothes, I chattered while walking away from the bathhouse into the dying sun, wondering what else could go wrong. Today I had burned my socks, got stymied on my route, been stuck in the mud and blown by the wind, and hauled my gear all over Cedar Key, and now the hot water had run out in the shower. Upon arriving at the campsite, I saw a bag sitting on the picnic table. Inside were pimento cheese sandwiches and fresh-baked cake, still warm to the touch. Deford's wife Janet had made the supper. This simple act renewed my spirit and made me grateful for what I had, rather than upset at getting stuck on Cedar Key.

Shortly after I awoke the next morning, Deford walked by with his dog and invited me over to meet his wife. I followed him into their fifth wheel, a cross between a camper and an RV, and met Janet. She had retired just two weeks earlier from being a nurse. I thanked her for the previous night's meal, and we sat down to a little breakfast and coffee. They convinced me to stick around Cedar Key for the day, offering the use of their bicycle to see the town and its history. In fact, concerning Cedar Key's history, I was duty-bound to explore it. Soon I was pedaling, not paddling, into town. I washed my clothes at Salty's Place. During the dry cycle I went over to the local canoe rental outfit, Nature Coast Canoe and Kayak Company. Terry was the proprietor. He had ended up on Cedar Key via Connecticut after making a "major lifestyle change" (read: quit stressful job in overcrowded city) and enjoyed living here. Terry gave me some helpful information about where to camp the next day. I explored the town a bit more. Most of the buildings were old wood-frame structures that gave the town a definite personality. There was a small public beach, a pier, and a marine biology station where several government agencies operated. There were no fast food restaurants, no big-box discount stores; nothing much above the tree line. In other words, Cedar Key still had charm. And the city fathers were going to keep it that way.

On Second Street was the Cedar Key Historical Society Museum, offering an overview of life here since Indian times. This piqued my interest in the place. Ironically, a hill nearby, where paved Second Street continued, was an old Indian shell mound.

History covered by asphalt. Oysters had their place here, but clamming had become the big industry. Clams have been a food source in Florida since the first Indian entered the peninsula but were not commercially gathered until the 1880s. Clamming took off when the massive clam beds of the Ten Thousand Islands were harvested, with a million taken in 1931 alone from a 150-square-mile area. Clammers often lived in shacks on the water, feeling for clams with their feet, which were covered in burlap to minimize cuts from shells.

By 1947, possibly as a result of freshwater diversion or a massive outbreak of red tide, the clam haven collapsed. Now clamming is closely regulated by the state, and a new form of clamming has evolved since 1993, as part of the larger movement toward aquaculture, the underwater farming of sea creatures. Farming clams involves three stages. First small seed clams are produced in a land-based hatchery. They are grown to a larger, plantable size in nurseries and then grown to harvest size on farms. These are underwater sections of coastal ocean bottom leased from the state. After the clams are harvested, they are washed, sorted, and graded at shellfish houses certified by the state, such as Nature Coast Industries.

Before modern clamming, there had been other extractive industries around Cedar Key. Fishing and oystering had had their day, the army had maintained a presence off and on, and lumber was important. As early as the 1830s, timber cruisers were stalking Florida for stands of cedar for the Faber Pencil Company. They came upon Cedar Key. Meanwhile, Cedar Key had become a supply depot for the U.S. Army. During the Civil War, the Rebels had salt works here. Salt was important for curing meat to feed the troops. After the war, Cedar Key became the pencil-making capital of the world. The trees that gave the island group its name—Cedar Key consists of several bridged islands—had soft wood conducive to pencil making. The industry grew wildly. Cedar Key saw its largest population, nearing two thousand people in the 1890s. But the nearly complete removal of cedar trees, along with the 1896 Hurricane, pretty much wiped out the industry. Today the clammers and other eclectic residents number around seven hundred. This is one of the few cities in Florida that is not at an all-time population high.

I was far from the first person to visit Cedar Key while exploring Florida. In 1867, the famed naturalist John Muir completed his Thousand Mile Walk, which became a book, here. He started in Kentucky and made his way down to Florida, ending at these islands he called "gems." He ended up staying for three months, not necessarily because he liked the place but because he was battling malaria. The tourism brochures leave out that part of the story.

The day stayed cold and the wind blew madly. While pedaling the bike, I surveyed the maze of oyster bars among the coastal islands. I wondered how I'd ever gotten through it all. Navigating is difficult among these low marsh islands and sometimes-submerged oyster bars. The islands don't give you readily identifiable landmarks that you can transpose to the nautical charts. They mainly look like endless sawgrass.

Later that afternoon, back at the Sunset Campground, one of the full-time residents, Bill Horn, came over to greet me. In his early sixties, with salt-with-pepper hair, a confident smile, and a big dose of vigor, he introduced himself. Originally from Jacksonville, he served twenty years in the navy and retired, traveling from Jacksonville to Cedar Key on fishing trips until he finally decided to make the move permanent. His full-time home was a trailer with a few outbuildings, fishing boats, and his dog Bear. He had converted one of his outbuildings into "guest quarters," which he offered me for the night. I took him up on it. It was going to be my first night inside four walls in a long while. Bill also served me supper, a roast he'd been cooking all day. The night headed below freezing again, and I didn't feel too guilty about enjoying the evening in a heated room. Bill was good company, the kind of un-foreseen pleasant surprise that is one element of an adventure.

I awoke at Bill's, chugged down some coffee, and loaded my gear. When I checked on the Kentuckians, Janet had breakfast go-ing—a good old southern breakfast of pancakes, bacon, toast, gravy, and coffee. I said good-bye to Bill, then Deford and Jan took me to the main ramp by the town park.

The sun was shining on the water and on us as Deford and Janet helped me unload their truck. I took a picture of them and their dog before sliding the kayak into the water. I placed the gear in the hatches, then jumped into the cockpit. Deford pushed me off and I sat up in the kayak to pull the spray skirt from under me. When I lifted my rear, my center of gravity became too high. The moving kayak veered left and over I went into the chilly water, scrambling out of the cockpit as soon as my trajectory was evident. The Gulf was only two feet deep here, but I sank up to my knees in mud, for a total wetting up to my waist. The wind cut right through my wet clothes as I stood up—red with embarrassment. This cer-tainly didn't enhance Deford and Janet's confidence in my making it to the Keys. The Kentuckians stood on the bank helpless, yet wanting to help. What was done was done. I calmly pulled out a water bottle and began methodically bailing out the cockpit. A chill crept into me. I got back in the sea kayak *very* carefully, attached the spray skirt to the cockpit, and paddled off toward Atsena Otie Key—not looking to see who was watching from the main boat ramp and pier. The folks at Cedar Key are probably still laughing at the paddler who said he was bound for the Keys. I myself was pre-pared to confiscate my own paddling credentials.

It was a short mile to Atsena Otie Key. I soon landed on the beach. Why Atsena Otie Key? In a word: history. The island was once the primary population center around here. To cut the chill I ran up the sandy spit to a dock. A foot trail left the dock and cut past an old pencil factory. Only the bricks remained. The island was abandoned in 1900 and has been uninhabited ever since. Farther on, I found the island cemetery, located high upon a hill, an old shell midden. I ran back to the boat to keep warming up, though the strong wind cut to the bone. This time my departure was uneventful, a major improvement over the previous embarkation. I paddled past Dog Island, wondering what story lay behind that name. Here I turned around and gave Cedar Key one last look. What serendipitous fortune it had been to have been stuck on Cedar Key, misadventures aside. The place exuded local history and passing it by would have been more than remiss. Life sometimes happens that way.

The now familiar water tower of Cedar Key shrank away into the distance. Birds flocked on the Corrigan Reefs, a series of sandbars east of Dog Island. The day remained sunny and cool. Farther down the shore, stakes were posted in the water, forming organized patterns. These were clam claims, aquaculture—the latest

The sun was shining on the water and on us, as Deford and Janet helped me unload their truck. I took a picture of them and their dog before sliding the kayak into the water.

Farther on, I found the island cemetery, located high upon a hill, an old shell midden.

way to make a living on Cedar Key. Perhaps these were worked by the boys from Nature Coast Industries.

The coast here ran east-west. Vast marsh grass savannas grew along the shore, extending inland a good distance to high, dry, and wooded terra firma. I paddled the shallow waters past Tripod Point, Kelly Creek, and Compass Point. The sun kept falling behind my back, and the wind picked up near the Waccasassa River. No suitable campsite was evident near the river mouth. Thousands of yards of marsh separated me from dry land. The wooded lands were just low lines of green on the horizon—at minimum, reaching the trees would be a hellish slog through the marsh grass. Continuous waves were banging the shore at the mouth of the river. Channel markers connected the river mouth to Waccasassa Bay. I paddled up the Waccasassa backlit by a low sun. Farther upriver was a campsite, according to Terry of the Nature Coast Canoe and Kayak Company. I wanted to get off the big water where the whole of Waccasassa Bay slammed into the river. A side creek, wooded on one bank, came in from the north. The other bank was marsh. I spontaneously abandoned Terry's suggestion and looked for a site up the side creek. Trees were plentiful, but the potential landings were not kayak friendly—too steep and muddy. A couple of hundred yards upstream there was a spot with overhanging cedar and a small live oak—there had to be dry ground up there. I pulled the Old Town alongside the vertical bank and decided the site looked good. Campsites always look better at the end of the day when you are tired.

I found enough flat ground for a camp among squat palms and some underbrush. The wooded area running alongside the creek averaged about thirty feet wide—on the far side marsh grass grew forth from mud. I pulled myself out of the boat and climbed cedar roots to reach the flat.

I changed after pulling the boat out of the water. Dry clothes felt good after being wet and fairly cold all day long. My wet falling-in-the-bay-at-Cedar-Key duds were hung on a palm in a dying sun. A snack and a little coffee warmed me up. I then relaxed and watched the day recede. The wind quit as if someone had hit a switch. A welcome silence hung over the mouth of the Waccasassa, especially welcome after hearing the moving air rush in my ears all day long. From this vantage point I could see across to wooded islands in the distance amid the marsh grass. A sense of isolation hung over the locale.

I leaned against a live oak and watched the blinking lights of the Crystal River nuclear plant at Yankeetown, sometimes checking the tide—it was now moving out. Even the blinking lights of the 456-foot cooling towers at the power plant evoked solitude. But there was a lot going on over there. Crystal River Nuclear Power Plant is part of Florida Power's Crystal River Energy Complex, one of the largest in the United States, producing enough power for 2 million Florida residents. Inside the nuclear plant uranium atoms were being split by neutrons, which produces heat, which creates steam, which turns turbines and generators to run people's TV sets in Tampa and heat their houses. My heat came from a little oak fire, capable of keeping one camper warm during the night, later supplemented with insulation from a sleeping bag.

The air cooled into the 40s, but I didn't mind, because this campsite would be a mosquito nightmare in warmer, wetter weather. And it can get really wet around here. Florida's most intense rain on record occurred at Yankeetown, a whopping 38.7 inches in 24 hours on September 5, 1950. Think about that the next time you are caught in a rainstorm. I arose early, revitalized the fire, and loaded in the dark to take advantage of the morning calm—the tide was once again going out and already pretty low. The drop down the mud bank from dry land to water had grown lengthier. In the dusky dawn I slid the loaded sea kayak about five feet down the bank into the creek. The boat hit the water, kept on going, and pulled me off the bank. I hung on to a cedar root with one hand and to the rope with the other, landing in the mud. My shoes went out of sight. But I did hang onto the boat. Getting into the kayak was turning into a Three Stooges sideshow. Slowly, slowly I worked my feet around, trying to get a little wiggle room, keeping one hand on the boat and the other on the root. My left foot popped out of the mud, minus a shoe. I slid my foot back into the hole and worked it out again, this time complete with shoe. The other came out about the same way. Before long I sat in the boat barefooted—after hanging the mud balls formerly known as shoes on the outside of the kayak. There's nothing like starting off the day's paddle with muck-laden shoes. Furthermore, the muck had now made it onto my hands, which I washed off.

Soon the small creek lay behind me and I entered the Wacca-sassa River. A porpoise heading upriver popped up just in front of the Old Town kayak. The most common porpoise in Florida waters is more accurately known as the bottlenose dolphin. Whales, dolphins, and porpoises are collectively known as cetaceans. They range in size from three feet in length to over eighty feet, some of the largest animals ever to have lived. A cetacean differs from a fish in may ways, the primary one being the way it obtains oxygen. Cetaceans rise to the surface to get air through a blowhole, whereas fish take oxygen directly from the water through gills. Fish have scales; cetaceans, ocean mammals, do not. Cetaceans have one dorsal fin and sometimes not even that. Fish have many fins. A fish swims by moving its head side to side, sending energy "waves" down its body to the tail, which also swings side to side and propels the creature through the water. Cetaceans swim with the help of powerful muscles in the rear third of the body, forcing the tail up and down, which propels the body through the water. Cetaceans are warm-blooded and give birth to live young; fish are cold-blooded and lay eggs.

The bottlenose dolphin is widely distributed around the world—cosmopolitan—and is highly active on the surface, riding the wakes and bow waves of boats, bodysurfing, and leaping far above the surface. Its dives typically last three to four minutes. Lone individuals sometimes seek out swimmers and small boats and may remain in the same area for years on end. It's hard to argue that these mammals don't play just for the sake of play, chasing each other, jumping in the air, following a boat, or seeking the company of a sea turtle. The one in the Waccasassa River seemed to be saying, "Hi."

The compass aimed south for Turtle Creek Point. I had to swing far into Waccasassa Bay to avoid the shoreline shallows. The cormorants standing in the shallows indicated waters that could not be paddled. I am surprised that Ponce De Leon did not call this peninsula "La Cormorant" instead of "La Florida." The double-crested cormorant is prevalent in Florida waters. It differs from other cormorants in its habit of taking shortcuts across land rather than nearly always flying over water.

Suddenly, from the east, a larger bird invaded the sky. A twin-rotor Coast Guard helicopter paralleling the shore veered my way, going directly overhead. I gave a thumbs up to indicate I was OK, and it passed on. The Old Town smoothly cruised over the grassy ocean floor beyond Porpoise Point, pushed by a couple of scrawny arms and an increasing wind. The Withlacoochee Reefs, a series of tidal sandbars, lay off to my left. I stayed away from them. The memories of Cedar Key were still vivid. In the distance ahead were channel markers indicating the Withlacoochee River, an altogether different body of water than the Withlacoochee River that merges with the Suwannee up north, though this river was supposedly named for that northern one. I kept forward, heading toward a series of east-west-running islands just beyond this second Withlacoochee. They had camping potential. These were spoil islands (a spoil island is made of material that has been dredged from the ocean floor to make a channel) from the never-completed Cross Florida Barge Canal. The intent had been for this waterway to connect the St. Johns River on the Atlantic to the Gulf of Mexico, enabling barges to go from the Atlantic to the Gulf in less time. The U.S. Army Corps of Engineers built part of the waterway meeting these specifications: at least 150 feet wide, with five locks 84 feet wide and 600 feet long, two dams, and numerous crossings of other canals.

Bisecting the Florida peninsula by canal was an idea that originated with the Spaniards. This would avoid the treacherous Florida Straits, where many a ship foundered on the rocks that lay perilously close to the Gulf Stream, the underwater current that took them back toward Europe. Nothing happened to bring the canal into being back then, but the idea persisted. In 1825, the governing body of the territory of Florida set up a canal committee and the U.S. Congress approved funds for the Corps of Engineers to plan a route.

A century passed. Then the Great Depression came. A canal across the state would benefit the Florida economy and would also provide jobs for the many unemployed, thought Roosevelt. By 1933 the Canal Authority of Florida had been created, and it started acquiring land. Two years later, FDR himself came down to set off the first blast, making a hole in the ground where water would flow to cross Florida. Less than a year later, the federal money ran out, and the project was halted with only 3 percent of the canal completed.

Interest in the canal waxed and waned, but in 1962 the Corps of Engineers again gave the go-ahead on the project. Now it would be a barge canal instead of a ship canal. The machines began digging in 1964, building the St. Johns Lock and damming the Ocklawaha River. Environmentalists mobilized, and opposition to the canal grew. One third of the project was completed this time; 70 million dollars had been spent by 1971, when Richard Nixon signed an executive order stopping the project. It took the bureaucrats and legislators until 1990 to deauthorize the project altogether, and the 110 miles of canal lands were given back to the state. Ironically enough, these lands have become the heart of the Cross Florida Greenway, a boon for nature lovers. The Ocklawaha River is slated to be restored and undammed.

Involvement in navigation projects by the Army Corps of Engineers dates back to the early days of the United States, when rivers and waterways were the primary means of travel and commerce. As the lands west of the original thirteen states began to be settled, rivers became even more important. They were the only practicable way to get through the vast forests and mountains of what was then the West. Henry Clay of Kentucky lobbied for federal assistance in maintaining the navigability of such waters. Others thought maintaining river navigability wasn't the job of the federal government. The Supreme Court settled it, ruling that the commerce clause of the Constitution enabled the federal government not only to regulate navigation and commerce but also make improvements in navigable waters. That gave birth to the Corps of Engineers, which began work on harbors, rivers, and waterways. For today's Florida, the Corps maintains deep draft harbors such as at Miami, Key West, Jacksonville, and Pensacola. Pleasure boaters see the Corps at work in the Intracoastal Waterway and on channels serving smaller rivers and inlets like at the Withlacoochee, Suwannee, and Cedar Key.

I pulled up for an inspection of one of the spoil islands marking the most westerly extension of this canal. This particular island was rocky limestone and very scrubby—mainly cactus and brush with a few ragged cedar trees. The spoil island looked as ugly as man-made islands should look. The term *spoil* may be the wrong word for this dredged material. Spoil implies useless material. But most of the dredged material is actually alluvial runoff: it used to be topsoil. When soil enters a waterway, it settles slowly, with heavier particles on the bottom. When this material is dredged to deepen a waterway, it is used not only to create spoil islands (they increase mangrove and saltmarsh areas) but also to renourish beaches and restore seagrass beds, and it is sold as marketable topsoil for use on land. This way the dredge material does not simply refill the channels. But the term *spoil* is here to stay.

I shunned the spoils and headed north into a relentless headwind, toward Chambers Island at the mouth of the Withlacoochee. Nearby were a boat ramp and a little park; I decided to check the park for drinking water. Vigilant kayakers are always trying to improve their limited water supply. A sign with two-foot-high letters outside the bathrooms said: "DO NOT DRINK THE WATER." I turned the knob on the spigot anyway and my nostrils were blown open by the odor of pure sulfur. Oh, well. I paddled back to Chambers Island and found a northeast-facing beach landing, out of the howling wind. I used the sun's warmth to dry my gear and clothes and to warm myself, as it was yet another cool day, cold in the wind. It had been so cold on this trip that at times I felt as if I was in a movie set of Florida, not in the real thing. Tallahassee holds the honor of having recorded the coldest temperature in the state, –2 degrees, in February of 1899.

My camp lay just a short distance from the Crystal River power plant, which had been on the horizon since Cedar Key. The plant had replaced the Cedar Key water tower as the current passage marker. On the far side of the island, facing the Withlacoochee River and the power plant, lay a broken and abandoned concrete foundation shaded by tall palms and oaks. Whatever this was, it had been here long before the power plant was ever built. The wind kept blowing beyond sunset—the wind was too strong to make a fire. To keep warm I put up the tent. It was the only way to get out of the wind. Normally I try to sleep out under the stars whenever possible. Also, if you camp out as much as I do, putting up and taking down any tent becomes an unpleasant chore. But when you really need one, a tent is a great thing to have. The lights of the power plant were visible through the tent window, blinking like some crazed temple to the gods of electricity, laughing at my being so close by yet not connected to the power grid, layered up inside the plastic enclosure.

It was 40 degrees at 5:30 A.M., and the wind still blew, though not like the night before. It was one of those dark mornings when you are reluctant to get out of the bag. I made a little fire to warm my hands after tightly closing the rubber storage bags and putting them in the Old Town's gear chambers. Off I paddled while the force of the tide pushed me out of the Withlacoochee River, rapidly passing channel markers in the tide-slimmed waterway while mud flats lay around head level. It was strange looking up at the sea floor that had been exposed by the low, low tide. The boat swung south past the spoil islands of the Cross Florida Barge Canal to the long continuous spoil bank emanating seaward from the Crystal River nuclear plant. The nautical chart indicated a breach in the spoil, but the Gulf and/or human neglect had closed the opening. It was a long way out to sea to get around the spoil. Waves were building here in Crystal Bay. I finally decided to paddle to a low spot on the spoil and pull the kayak over to the other side. A portage of sorts was required to get across. Portaging is hauling your boat overland from one body of water to get to the next body of water. I had done lots of portaging in Minnesota's Boundary Waters Canoe Area Wilderness, but in Florida the exercise was quite different. The waves were splashing the Old Town as I pulled the craft over the bulk of the spoil, a distance of about eighty feet over land to the far side and ten feet high at its maximum. It wasn't long before I returned to the water, entering Crystal Bay below high thin clouds veiling the sun.

In the distance I spotted some limestone rocks protruding above the water. Perched pelicans and cormorants had alerted me from afar. I negotiated the surrounding water and pulled the boat onto the rocks as the birds scattered to float atop the sea. These shallows can be a blessing or a curse—a blessing when it is time to stop; but a curse when it is so shallow that your boat gets stuck. Beyond the rocks I kept south, staying far from shore—away from more shallow water. Seagrasses, corals, sponges, porpoises, and fish of all kinds plied the translucent waters below. Seagrasses are not only attractive but also important to the health of marine waters. But clear waters are important for seagrasses, since they need light for photosynthesis. An estimated half-million acres of seagrasses grow in the coastal waters of Florida, stabilizing the sea bottom much as grass prevents erosion on land, trapping fine sediments and particles. These grasses are important for sea life, acting as a nursery for fish, crustaceans, and shellfish. That is why propeller boats are encouraged to be careful while traveling through shallow waters underlain with seagrass.

To the west, the Crystal River flowed into the Gulf. The Crystal River flows for a mere seven miles from its source to the Gulf, but is very important to wildlife, especially manatees. When winter chills the Gulf waters, as many as two hundred manatees migrate up the Crystal River to Kings Bay, where Crystal Springs keeps the waters relatively warm. This the largest wintertime concentration of manatees in the United States, one place in Florida where manatee activity is increasing. But the massing in the river may signal troubled waters elsewhere.

Beyond Crystal Bay were the St. Martins Keys, where I hoped to find a camp. Among the islands there were mud flats and birds. The nautical chart proved accurate in showing all the shallow water out here, some of which would need to be traversed to reach the islands. Luckily, the tide was rising. A Gulf paddler's passage depends on the rise and fall of the tides. For that matter, all seafarers and those who make their living off the salty sea must be more attuned to tides than to clocks.

Out here, the air lay still and the ocean spread eerily flat—a bland pale sky reflected off the water, melding water and sky into one white haze. Herons and egrets fed in the distance. I turned the rudder of the Old Town westward to deeper water and followed the rising tide as it seeped into the close-knit group of islands. The nautical chart showed one of the St. Martins Keys to be Sand Key. Surely I would find a beach landing and campsite on Sand Key. I drifted slowly toward the island. But there was no visible sand on Sand Key—things must have changed since it was named. Or perhaps it was wrongly named. I pulled up to the mud and walked onto land so wet that it barely qualified as land—the land resembled chocolate pudding. Behind some patchy grass were black mangroves, their air-gathering roots or pneumatophores rising from the brown muck. A man's hind end would be wet inside a minute if he sat down here. I walked to the southeast end of the island, a less likely to a place for a campsite since it didn't face seaward. Seaward locations sometimes receive a buildup of sand from wave action. But there was no sand and nowhere to camp. Furthermore, the waters were so shallow that the outgoing tide was likely to strand me for hours the following morning. After seven hours of paddling I yearned for a camp, but I gave up on the St. Martins Keys. They were for the birds.

Where to go? East, toward Shell Island at the mouth of the Homosassa River, I decided. Shell Island had to be high and dry. But someone had beaten me to it—a house on pilings stood there. I tiredly paddled inland up the Homosassa River, blindly hoping for a campsite. This river resembled the Crystal River; a spring-fed waterway running a short piece to the Gulf. Just a half mile beyond Shell Island and directly along the river was another island of shell. It had no name on the nautical chart but was undoubtedly an Indian midden. Live oaks, palm, and cedar grew atop the shell bank, which stood ten feet high. The exposed shells formed a little beach that made for an easy landing. I toted the gear up the mound, sponged water out of the boat cockpit, and gathered wood for an evening fire. Beyond the shell island a few palm islands were scattered in the salt marsh. A couple of fishing boats headed out to sea around sunset. An advantage to camping here along the Homosassa, or any other river for that matter, is the depth of the river. The tides won't leave you stranded. The fire burned out quickly, and so did I. The time to travel, to see Florida by water, was by day. Soon I settled into my sack, watching shooting stars compete for regard against the blur of the Milky Way and millions of other worlds. My lids closed and it was morning again before I knew it.

Up at 5 A.M.—another eye-appealing Florida sunrise. Sunrise and sunset are some of the best times to be outside, to watch the colors of the sky and light change, alternately revealing and concealing the world around you. I caught the outgoing tide on the Homosassa. The maw of the Gulf opened up. I had spent the night in Citrus County, where not many oranges are grown. Citrus boomed in the 1800s, but the Great Freeze of 1894–95 killed most of the trees here. The county had been founded just a few years earlier in 1887. Then phosphate was discovered and mined, helping restore the economy. Germany bought the most phosphate. But the United States quit trading with the Germans during World War I. The economy went south again. Today, much of the county's economy is based on outdoor recreation; the nuclear plant is the biggest employer.

A flock of birds bobbed on the water's surface ahead. There seemed to be a lot of commotion and squawking. Upon closer inspection I saw a couple of fins above the water. What was going on? Was it a shark? No, a couple of porpoises were swimming in a circle among the birds. The birds would dive down as if they were chasing the porpoises. Probably they were all battling for minnows or some other yummy fare corralled by the dolphins. An altogether natural slaughter was occurring. Fishermen look for such surface feeding and try to determine what is driving the little fish up, and from which direction, so that they can fish there, getting in on the action.

I made my way around Chassahowitzka Point to enter Chassahowitzka Bay, coming to a long line of poles in the water. From a distance, the poles resembled channel markers. They were the northern boundary markers of the Chassahowitzka National Wildlife Refuge. This 31,000-acre enclave, established in the 1940s, is known as a major wintering ground for ducks and coots. The lightly visited refuge is accessible only by boat.

Lately, the refuge has become the chosen winter home of endangered whooping cranes. Only about four hundred of the birds are known to exist. For decades only a single flock of whooping cranes made the twice-yearly migration, summering in northwestern Canada and wintering in Texas. Now a new flock that summers in Wisconsin has begun to spend winters on Florida's Chassahowitzka, having been led there by an ultralight plane, of all things. Here's how it works. As chicks, the cranes were trained to follow an ultralight aircraft with V-shaped wings, piloted by a man in a giant gray crane costume. Anyone interacting with the birds wears a costume. There is no direct human-crane interaction. The birds flew migration legs ranging from twenty to ninety miles per day. At each stop on the route, the birds were placed in pens to keep them away from people. The program seems to be working. A test flock of cranes was led to Florida during fall, and the birds flew back to Wisconsin on their own in spring, then returned to Chassahowitzka on their own the following fall. All concerned fervently hope that this wildlife refuge will become a long-term refuge for the cranes.

As the sun rose, the ocean flattened, mirroring the indistinct white sky. Once again sky and water melded into one. It was as if I was paddling off the edge of a blank canvas. All was still around the boat. The sea grass below the waterline lay just as still. I paddled on, stopping ahead near Saddle Key on a rock outcrop. After docking the boat, I made lunch atop the kayak. There were no human sights or sounds anywhere—silence reigned. A scent of smoke from inland wildfires drifted over the water. They were probably in Marion County, home of the Ocala National Forest.

Beyond Saddle Key, stingrays were swimming in the shallows. Their flat beige bodies were well camouflaged against the sand. Sometimes they would swim away quickly; at other times they lay half covered in the sand, waiting for prey. There were living and decaying shells, sometimes with bodies visible, clinging to the ocean floor. I was snorkeling without a mask.

Time and progress slowed neared the town of Bayport. Pine Island, complete with houses, seemed to stand still to the west. The end of a paddling day happens like that. The tide was coming up, so I chanced getting stuck and beelined through shallow water to the mouth of the Weeki Wachee River, another spring-fed, relatively short watercourse with a great name. Florida's Indians didn't have a written language, but they did work up some names that are hard to spell.

A pier stretched over the water. People were milling around, watching boats come and go or just looking out over the ocean. I paddled close to ask someone about drinking water and camping, but before I could ask my first question, a woman addressed me: "Are you lost?"

"No," I replied, wondering whether my face harbored some confusion. I asked her my questions, and she launched into the other normal questions—where are you from, where are you going, etc., which I answered. She told me to pull around the pier to a nearby dock. I did.

At the dock, she and her friend quizzed me further, and then she excitedly said, "I've got to get Tom." I didn't know who Tom was, but he sounded pretty important and might know something I needed to hear. The water question had already been answered—a fountain stood by the dock. I waited for Tom and watched a Game and Fish Commission officer write people tickets for having no life jackets, for improper papers, and for other boating violations. It was a Saturday. Boats were coming and going, and everyone was enjoying the refreshing sunny day, except those getting tickets. It felt good to be standing up and I wasn't in any hurry to go anywhere, having stroked the blade all day long. Tom arrived in a blue Chevy Suburban, Florida gazetteer in hand, as I listened to another ticket victim explain why she shouldn't be given a ticket. Tom stood tall and healthy in his early seventies and carried a certain organized air about him. He immediately demonstrated his analytical mind while using carefully measured words to offer me camping suggestions. He was an avid kayaker himself and had longed to explore more of Florida's Nature Coast. Together we glanced at the gazetteer and visited further on the dock. He then concluded by inviting me to stay with his group. I was taken aback yet intrigued. They were friendly and surely could tell me more about the area than I could learn from a book. But I was dirty and not wanting to impose myself on them. When folks are camping together out in the woods or on the waterways, all are at the same general dirtiness level, so being less than clean doesn't matter. This clan was all well scrubbed. I could smell their soap-scented selves. However, the spirit of spontaneous adventure ruled the day and I took them up on the invitation.

There were seven of them in all staying at Tom's house, a weekend house, up the road. The whole group hailed from the same neighborhood in Clearwater, Florida, south of Bayport. We loaded my boat onto his Suburban and soon I met the rest of the crew, hereafter known as the Clearwater Seven. Tom's wife Mary Ann, who had asked in her soft South Georgia accent if I was lost, sent me to the shower. I was grateful, though a little embarrassed. The other women—Heather, Elsa, and Sally—were preparing supper.

After cleaning up, I joined the fellows in a game of Washers-in-the-Hole. The game is like inverted horseshoes—you toss huge washers into holes in a box rather than trying to ring a horseshoe around a stake. My partner was Rick, a well-groomed Clearwater lawyer with a literary bent. His hair always looked well put together, even when he was dressed as casually as he was now, in jeans and a neatly tucked-in flannel shirt. A native Floridian, Rick had seen his state change in many ways, primarily getting more crowded. Our competitors were Tom and Derik, formerly of England. Derik still had the accent. His skillful tossing of the washer backed up his confident air. Rick and I were the youngest of the crowd but were taking a whipping at the hands of the elders. I was cussing the entire British citizenry under my breath with each of Derik's accurate landings of the washer.

We loaded my boat onto his Suburban and soon I met the rest of the crew, hereafter known as the Clearwater Seven.

Later we all ate steaks, baked potatoes, salad, and even a cake, as it was Sally's birthday. Sally was a lawyer too and lived right across the street in Clearwater from Tom and Mary Ann. On Sally's behalf, we all wore little birthday hats at the dinner table. Just hours before, I couldn't have pictured myself in this situation in a million years! After dinner Tom, a sage of sea kayaking, delivered a few paddling pointers. His stroke ideas would prove invaluable on down the line.

Bayport still had a relaxed feel. Founded in the 1840s at the mouth of the Weeki Wachee River, Bayport grew around its Gulf access, which was used for fledgling Hernando County to ship its cotton and cattle, despite the area's shallow waters on the Gulf. The importance of the place was not lost on the Confederates during the Civil War; they used Bayport for trade as the Union had blockaded larger Gulf ports. Hernando Countians were loyal to the South, even before the War between the States. Originally named after Hernando De Soto, the county was later renamed Benton, after the Missouri senator Thomas Hart Benton. But then he opposed the Compromise of 1850, which admitted California as a free state but allowed interstate slave trade; the residents changed the name of their county back to Hernando.

Word leaked out about Bayport and federal forces twice raided the town, looting homes and burning the town docks. After the war, Bayport became Hernando County's major shipping center until the railroad came to Brooksville in 1885, effectively ending the shipping era here, much as the metal tracks had undone the steamboats on the Suwannee. Efficiency won again.

After the war, Bayport reverted to a backwater. Rumrunners took advantage of the quiet, bringing booze ashore. They would then repack it in peanut cartons and ship it inland for resale. Modern conveniences made their way to Bayport in the 1950s, including the phone and electricity. Growth pressure has increased; that's why many are happy about recent land purchases by the Southwest Florida Water Management District, reducing developable land.

The next morning we enjoyed an English breakfast, as suggested by Derik. His wife Heather, a real estate agent, had an appealing confidence about her, too. Funny how when describing people, you often focus on what they do for a living, their work, as revealing who they are. And when you meet people, the question "What do you do?" usually comes up early in the conversation. Some people are defined by their jobs. My work and I are inseparable. Others may prefer to be defined by their hobbies, say someone who works in a nuclear plant but loves to scuba dive. It must be in the nature of the job. A pro football player probably doesn't mind being defined by his job, whereas a trash collector might.

On my departure, Heather gave me a St. Christopher medal. It protects the traveler—he is the patron saint of travelers. I hoped it would help. The group escorted me to the dock and Tom helped me load up. We said good-bye, those dreaded good-byes, and I was on my way, paddling south, heading south into the most populous end of the state. My general direction was reflecting the state's growth pattern, from north to south. Yet today, the south is the most populous and the north has become the quiet part of the state. Now, many Sunshine Staters are heading to northern Florida to escape the congestion of the south.

The ocean soon became mine again as the shallows prevented motorboats from going to most of the stretches I was paddling. Motor boaters had to ply the channels between the mainland and the deeper ocean, miles from shore, to do any wide-open boating. The waters around Round Island were too shallow even for a sea kayak. I got out of the boat, walking the sandy bottom, and pulled the craft a short distance to deeper water. It didn't matter; I was enjoying the freedom, sunshine, and warmth. Once I was back in the boat, the sun bore down on my bare arms as I paddled over the visible sea floor. Numerous limestone outcrops projected above the water surface. On the shore stood Hernando Beach, the first heavily populated shoreline. It had to happen sooner or later. I made eight easy miles from Bayport to Horse Island. From a bird's point of view, the isle did bear a rough resemblance to an equine. Mangrove covered most of Horse Island, save for one section of higher ground where a long shell mound harbored palm, cedar, saffron-plum, and too much Brazilian pepper. A small rock landing led to a larger limestone outcrop that led to the mound, a few feet above shore. Anglers had made a little table on the mound and left a limestone fire ring.

Someone had also collected and assembled several horseshoe crab shells and laid them in a row at the campsite. A premade camp. I could handle that. The horseshoe crab is one of the most ancient animals in the Gulf. Not actually a crab at all, it is related to the extinct trilobites that once dominated the seas. Its closest living relatives are the land-based scorpions and spiders. Its long tail is used to balance the creature and for burrowing in the sand. Horse-

On my departure, Heather gave me a St. Christopher medal. It protects the traveler. I hoped it would help.

shoe crabs feed on worms and soft-bodied creatures in shallow sand-bottomed water.

A bearded fellow in a little sailing dinghy hollered out as he passed. He looked around fifty. He was from Maine, and his name was Terry. I didn't ask what his job was. He had moved down here and had built his own boat—the dinghy he sailed. In his New England accent he asked me the usual questions, then one more that was sometimes asked. Did I have a gun? Not with me, I told him, though I have a gun at home. What would I need a gun for out here—an inconsiderate motorboater? Why would someone want to fool with a sea kayaker? It would take too much work to get into a boat and come and find me. Bad guys could rob someone from the convenience of their car. Honestly, I never considered bringing a gun. It would just be something else to keep dry. But it really came down to a question of point of view. Some see potential danger everywhere. I tend to believe I can handle just about any situation that comes along. Call it self-confidence; call it the personal fable. Much of it derives from going on trips alone and handling whatever does come my way. Anyway, most people are too busy with their own lives to go messing with mine. Now, if I were floating the high seas, or backpacking in Alaska's grizzly country, or living in downtown Detroit, I might be more inclined to carry a gun. But I had not met or seen the first person along the way who seemed to pose any threat.

Terry had camped here on Horse Island before and lately had heard about some folks digging around on the shell mound, looking for artifacts. Indeed, there were small squared-off holes in the ground. I hoped they wouldn't dig it all up. Had it not been for the shell mound, neither Terry nor I nor anyone else could have camped on Horse Island. The island would have been a mangrove mud hole like Sand Key in the St. Martins Keys.

That evening the sea lay flat and all became quiet. I watched the land roll toward night from my mound perch. The eastern horizon was lined with stars dotting an inky black sky; overhead only the brightest celestial bodies had penetrated the dusk. Day drowned in darkness along the western heavens. I was waiting for serenading violins to complete the picture. Suddenly an airboat raced by so loudly that it actually vibrated the land—putting those cars with huge bass speakers that teenagers drive to shame. Ear pollution.

A crackling mangrove fire lit up the night, emitting its strange but customary mustard-yellow flame. Pioneers lit "punks," or "smudges," as these small, smoky fires of black mangrove were known, as a natural bug repellent. The scent of the mangrove fire drifted my way, kindling up memories of nights camping on the Gulf beaches of Everglades National Park. The mangrove has its own particular smell, as do the cedar fires I had enjoyed farther up the coast. Earlier still, on the Suwannee River, pine fires had made our campsites fragrant. Crickets sang in the night; fish occasionally jumped, chasing each other in the never-ending cycle of life and death in the salt water. The warm night fell heavy with dew; drops gathered on all my gear.

The lights of Greater Tampa illuminated the southern sky. The Nature Coast had ended around Bayport. I wasn't particularly desirous of all the civilization to the south. More people would mean more opportunities to meet interesting people, but more people would also mean more anonymity, translating into less friendly people. When acquaintances learn of my lifestyle, the question of being alone always comes up. I have never minded being alone. Having somebody, anybody, around, just to be around somebody doesn't work for me. I have several close, long-term friends. It takes effort to stay friends, worthwhile effort, but we do things when we can. The problem is that doing what I do *requires* great amounts of solitude. For starters, who can leave current commitments to pick up and go somewhere for months at a time? Who has the time, money, or desire to go and hike five hundred miles of trails somewhere and write a book about it, or spend the winter paddling the Everglades then write a book about it, or go tent camping all over Colorado then write a book about it? Second, writing is a solitary game. It demands solitude. Two people can't sit together pecking on a keyboard. That doesn't make sense. Third, I was content. During all the solitude I had already experienced, I had come to accept myself and my place in the world. I know myself upside down, inside out, and backwards. Many postmodern adults spend way too much time on self-absorption, thinking about personal foibles, troubles, and demons, but I know full well that all the most fascinating things in the world are beyond what lies inside my own skull. That is a huge element of any trip—to see what's out there. I was about to pitch headlong into serious urbanization.

The Urban Coast

I left Horse Island, heading southwest into a light wind. The only sounds were the stroke, dip, and swish of the double-bladed paddle. The kayak gracefully cut through the sea, leaving a symmetrical wake. I concentrated on the task at hand, self-propelled progress on the salty sea. To navigate, I would figure a compass heading for where I needed to go from the nautical chart. Then I would find a fixed object in the distance in that direction and paddle for it. That way there was less need to keep looking down at the compass. Paddle passage is slow, and in wide-open waters there is less need to check your position constantly on the nautical charts. The fixed object might be an island in the distance, a channel marker, a rock outcrop, or a building. Spoil islands and dredged channels were definite passage points that I would correlate on the nautical charts and in the water. It was relieving to stop, get out of the kayak, and take a break on those spoil islands, which ranged from a few rocks barely above the water to several acres of trees and land.

Farther down the coast a few fishing shacks stood on pilings, perhaps a mile off the coast in shallow water. Birds perched on most of them—some of the buildings were used, others were past use. Some shacks were plain gone. Rotted pilings reached from the Gulf with nothing left to support. I took a break at nearby Durney Key. South winds warmed the day and blew right in my face, picking up by the minute and blocking progress. My goals became segmented—Durney Key to Green Key and take a paddle break out of the wind. Rest my arms. Green Key to Gulf Harbor— refold the nautical chart. Gulf Harbor to Bailey's Bluff—the coast was lined with large houses, some of them huge, impressive three- and four-story mansions. Beyond Bailey's Bluff was a large power plant and park, where the curious looked down at manatees warming in the plant's water discharge.

The Anclote Keys lay to my right. Just beyond here the marked channel of the Anclote River led into Tarpon Springs, once known for its sponges. Anson Safford, former governor of Arizona, founded the town of Tarpon Springs in 1882. A fellow named John Cheyney began pulling natural sponges from the sea floor with a hook from his boat. In 1905, Greek families came here and began sponging a different way, diving for the sea creatures, taking them by hand. Soon Tarpon Springs became the sponge capital of the world. In the late 1930s a disease spread through the sponge beds, wiping out the population. By the time the beds came back, plastic sponges had made the natural sponges obsolete. Environmentalists might have a hard time picking out which is the sorrier course: extracting sponges from the sea, or extracting oil for plastic to manufacture sponges that don't decay away, then having all those used sponges end up in dumps. Either way the consumer, and I'm one of them, demands and uses sponges.

The Gulf Coast Intracoastal Waterway began at the mouth of the Anclote River. Just beyond the Anclote stood a large spoil island, near Brady Island. I paddled alongside the spoil and spied a camp. I paddled up to a beach beside a homemade dock and immediately unloaded my gear onto a banquet table and a thirty-foot-long picnic table, both of which stood under a tin roof that had seen better days. Black mangrove rimmed the sandy island, while Australian pine and Brazilian pepper, along with a few palms, shaded the interior. It seemed somehow fitting that an exotic spoil island made from channel dredging would sport all this exotic vegetation.

Australian pines are not true pines. They are members of the beefwood family and were introduced to Florida as windbreaks and beauty strips. The "needles" you see on the branches are actually tiny scale-like leaves. This small size helps each leaf conserve heat and water. Their efficiency is destructive—they invade and take over areas of native vegetation, accomplishing this by shading out other trees and dropping their branchlets onto the ground, releasing chemicals that suppress growth of other trees.

The U.S. Department of Agriculture in 1898 introduced Brazilian pepper, an obvious native of Brazil, into Florida. Originally an ornamental plant known for its bright red berries, it has propagated far and wide through the southern part of the peninsula. It forms nearly impenetrable thickets in flatwoods, hammocks, and, as on this island, on the landward edge of mangrove fringes. Birds love the berries, especially mockingbirds, robins, and cedar waxwings. Their droppings have been a primary spreader of the Brazilian pepper. The tree grows well in full sun and is hard to eradicate once it is fully established. Some Florida natives argue that this tree is rather like the Yankees that flock here . . .

I ate supper on the dock, watching the sun fall behind an incoming bank of clouds. The days were certainly getting longer. Many boats were tooling around in the ensuing dark. One curved right around the island, a jet ski, speeding with no lights, and al-most hit a well-lit boat heading down the main channel into Tar-

I paddled up to a beach beside a homemade dock and immediately unloaded my gear onto a banquet table and a thirty-foot-long picnic table, both of which stood under a tin roof that had seen better days.

pon Springs. Bad boaters can give all boaters a bad reputation in the eyes of the owners of self-propelled craft. I try to view them on a case-by-case basis; I didn't come here to be the marine police.

The warm evening grew windy. Another tough pull lay ahead the next day. When I awoke during the night, the Australian pines were whooshing back and forth in the sky, raising my concern about the next day. I tried to minimize the impact of the wind by getting up early before the sun's heat exacerbated the gusts. I was in the cockpit and on the water while darkness still lay over the roaming sea. A stiff breeze came from the south. After departing the spoil island, keeping on the Intracoastal Waterway, I remember thinking how strong the wind was as I strained to paddle into it. I began just trying to make short-distance goals. By 10:00 A.M., I reached Indian Bluff Island, listening to the gusts peal in my ears, thinking how light the wind had been earlier. Rick Nail of the Clearwater Seven expected me in downtown Clearwater for lunch at noon. The Intracoastal Waterway went right past his office, just a block from the water. A timely arrival seemed unlikely as downtown stood a good seven miles distant. Hugging the shore didn't minimize the wind; the gusts were simply too strong and getting stronger by the minute. Even the barrier islands forming the westward edge of St. Joseph Sound—Honeymoon Island and Caldesi Island—offered no relief. The wind tore straight up the sound. A causeway, which did cut down on the waves, connected the mainland and Honeymoon Island ahead. A bridge divided the causeway toward the middle of the sound. I paddled under the bridge, which hummed with traffic. Once south of this bridge I was in waves of three feet and more, and coming one after another, slamming over the boat and into my chest. Once again I made directly for the shore.

Houses lined the shoreline, but the residents couldn't help me with my problem. I bounced along the coastline, sometimes going beneath the piers of the houses that extended into the sound from sea walls. It was likely around noon. My camera had a clock on it, but I couldn't stop to look at it, or the boat would turn sideways to the wind and something bad might happen after that.

Strangely enough, I spotted a phone booth up a side street from the water. The urban coast. I indulged in the absurdity of imagining a Calusa Indian calling his buddy down on Key Largo to see if the fish were biting. I pulled the boat out and climbed into life on the streets beside Clearwater Bay, walking a block to the pay phone to call Rick. A small motel stood at the corner near the pay phone. I walked over to an older woman ordering a man around while they were cleaning rooms. In the most sensible-sounding voice I could muster, I asked them, "Where am I?"

The woman gave me a "you freak" look but replied, "Dunedin." I wonder what she would have thought if I had still had my spray skirt on. For some reason I didn't feel like explaining having gotten here by boat. The man, her order taker, glanced over his shoulder and pushed the little clean-up cart to the next room. I could feel their vibes of misery from across the parking lot. Once in the phone booth I shut the door, cutting down on the traffic noise from the adjacent street, and called Rick. From the booth I could look into the open door of one room. While talking to Rick on the phone, I watched a woman who was likely a prostitute get ready for the day. She finally walked out in the shortest pants you could imagine that could still be called pants. She walked toward the pay phone and gave a haughty look, then walked back to her room and closed the door. Apparently, I was tying up her phone line.

Rick wasn't surprised that the wind had slowed my progress. I relayed my position to him. He called Tom and Mary Ann and the whole gang. They were all soon in Dunedin, loading my stuff on top of Tom's car. The four of us had lunch at Sam's, enjoying mullet sandwiches. The wind was nil inside the restaurant. I gave up paddling for the day, having made eight miles in five and a half hour of paddling. That night, the Clearwater Seven gathered once again at Tom's house for pizza and a little conversation. The weather service predicted rain and heavy wind the next day, so I decided to lay over and rest up. Tom and Mary Ann were willing to put up an out-of-state paddler.

Rick took me on a tour of Clearwater the next day and gave me a little history lesson along the way. A fellow named Philippe first settled the area. After facing Indians on the east coast of Florida, the Frenchman had received a hot land tip from a pirate who told of the beautiful waters of the area. Philippe landed east of Clearwater on the Pinellas Peninsula, where he established a plantation. It was on his plantation that citrus was planted in rows for the first time. His idea remains popular.

Under the 1842 Armed Occupation Act, the area began to be settled. This act was intended to bring Americans to southern Florida, effectively outnumbering the Seminoles. It gave 160 acres of land to any settler who would "bear arms and live on the land in a fit habitation for five years and cultivate at least five acres." Over thirteen hundred grants were handed out here. Many of these folks saw the high bluff and freshwater springs of what is now Clearwater as an ideal location. Judging by the current state of Pinellas County, which is the most urbanized county in Florida, people have been locating here ever since.

Later that evening the Clearwater Seven assembled at Rick's house for a delicious Italian meal. We ate in the dining room, which had an Italian motif, reflecting Rick's ancestry. His wife Elsa had put the room together. It was another reflection of her classy sense of style, which showed through whether she was decorating a room, wearing an outfit, or setting the table upon which we ate chicken cacciatore.

In the morning I put in back near the hotel and phone booth at Dunedin, right where I had taken out two days earlier. Tom had decided to accompany me through the Clearwater area, paddling one of his kayaks. Mary Ann and their daughter Leslie bid us goodbye. Leslie shot a few photos as Tom and I paddled south on a flat bay beneath warm and leaden skies. At least the wind wasn't blowing in our faces at twenty miles per hour. We kept south through Clearwater Harbor, with aquamarine waters as beautiful as the pirate promised Philippe. The easy stroking across the still water contrasted greatly with the paddling two days earlier. I enjoyed once again having a paddle partner. Tom demonstrated some strokes for me and pointed out more Clearwater landmarks. A point of pride for area residents is the Belleview Biltmore. This hotel, built by railroad magnate Henry Flagler and claiming to be the largest wood structure in the world, opened in 1897. Situated among the oaks on the Clearwater Bluff, it became a playground for the elite. The hotel fell into disrepair over time, culminating in a four-year stint as barracks for the U.S. Air Force. Then the 244 rooms were vacant. After passing through a few other hands, the Biltmore has since been restored and is now on the National Registry of Historic Places.

A light mist began to fall, the kind that doesn't rush you to grab your rain jacket but eventually soaks you just the same. It worked its magic on us. Tom ended his journey at the Belleair Bridge, getting a shuttle ride from Mary Ann. I headed south and south again, then east into the Narrows, a slender watery passage on the Intracoastal Waterway between the mainland and Indian Rocks Beach. The rain ceased, but the air hung heavy and limp like a wet blanket, as opposed to the crisp and sweet air of the cold fronts that had passed through earlier in the adventure. The spans over the Narrows were now of the drawbridge variety, opening in the center to allow passage of large boats like cabin cruisers and sailboats. I passed below the drawbridges low and quiet.

To maximize water access, many bayside waterfront developments were created with fill and then built into the water, creating artificial land where more folks could cram their houses along the water. *Waterfront.* The magic word. Homeowners boast of it and real estate agents tout it. Florida has around 8,500 miles of coastline, but that figure is increasing all the time. Waterfront adds value, and the Pinellas County tax assessor's office loved that. Most of these properties were all house and very little yard. If the person in house A sneezes, the person in House B says, "Bless you." And these were big expensive houses. High-rises also dotted the landscape. This way they could look over the water and really didn't have much less yard than the homeowners. But the homeowners had docks. And the docks were important for boating, so that they could all get out on the water any given Sunday and try to run over each other, transferring the rush, rush, rush mentality of the roadways to the waterways. The situation became this simple: too many people in too little space.

This section was no wilderness adventure. It was a bad lesson in urban planning. Or a good lesson, depending on your point of view. If you are going to urbanize an area, why not increase the density to its absolute maximum carrying capacity? This way the negative effects of overurbanization are concentrated. Luckily for me, an uninhabited spoil island lay a little south of the Narrows. It had a shell and sand beach that made for the all-important ready landing, and many pines for wind and shade protection, as the day had turned partly sunny. I made the most unwild camp ever in my life, across from several of those fill-'em-up and jut-'em-out housing developments. It was about a quarter to half a mile across northern Boca Ciega Bay to these homes. Hell, it wasn't as if there was anywhere wild to camp around here anyway. So, I accepted the reality of Pinellas County in the twenty-first century.

The nighttime fire lit the encampment as I watched a paper and foil noodle package ignite in a dark cloud. Which was better—to burn trash, handing it over to the mercy of the four winds, or to let it pile up in a landfill, a memorial to the waste of modern times? Back in the late '60s, my elementary school had an incinerator, just off the playground. It had a towering smokestack. I wondered what went into that incinerator? Broken rulers, bent protractors, 'flu-inspired vomit, swept up with that dry stuff they put on it to clean it up, cafeteria mess, little colored drawings, colored paper, cutouts of pilgrims and turkeys. Clarence, the school janitor, must have known the secrets of the old incinerator.

Obviously, the burial rite is in favor today. On the outskirts of every town, places politely known as landfills have telltale pipes dug into them, to let the methane escape as the discarded waste rots beneath seeded grass mounds. More air pollution. It's not easy to get authorization to build a new landfill now, but who can

I made the most unwild camp ever in my life, across from several of those fill-'em-up and jut-'em-out housing developments.

blame a community for not wanting one in their midst? What's the answer? Recycling can only go some of the way in reducing the amount of waste entering landfills.

After supper my headlamp went out. The bulb died. I put in the spare bulb. It flashed then immediately went out. The gas lantern I had been using had a broken globe, and I was out of mantles. A half moon and the lights of the surrounding urban area helped me get around but weren't sufficient for cooking. I decided to use a tried-and-true camping trick. First, I found an old soup can and stuffed it with paper (cloth also works). Then I poured Coleman fuel into the can. This fuel is really just ultraclean gasoline, which I was using to run the stove and lantern. As volatile as the fuel is, you would think it would immediately ignite, but if the paper is packed tightly enough, the fuel burns slowly, putting out a flicker-ing flame that will work for light in a pinch. Perhaps it would also keep the rats at bay. At least while I ate. That's right, rats. There are rats on some of these spoil islands. Those disgusting skitterbugs were running around in the brush, occasionally crossing open areas where their dark figures were visible against the lighter sand.

That night a heavy fog moved in and diffused the moonlight, adding an eerie pall to the oceanscape. In the distance, cars and trucks rattled across the Tom Stuart Causeway. I slept in the open as usual; betting that the rats wouldn't hunger for a little ear lobe during the night. In warmer months, the number of nights I would have spent out in the open would have been reduced to zero due to biting insects. That was one of the reasons I chose winter for the trip. Even at this time of year, it was only a matter of precipitation and warmth before the bugs started back up in this part of the state.

The fog thickened by early morning. I took off at daylight and was soon admitting to myself this was an occasion when the channel markers of the Intracoastal Waterway were a blessing. They made navigation easier. Furthermore, the motorboats stayed in, making this foggy paddle less treacherous. I stroked through calm waters, hardly aware of all the houses lining the bay. Passing under the bridges was as noisy as ever. Overhead, everybody seemed in a hurry. They probably were. It's called "rush hour." Hurrying isn't an option in a sea kayak. Your only speeds are slow and a little faster than slow. To slow down your lifestyle, paddling is the surefire remedy.

The wind came out of nowhere in the Pass-A-Grille Channel. Now that's a good name, Pass-A-Grille. Perhaps it means "get-through-before-you-get-cooked." The open Gulf lay to my right, though it wasn't visible through the dense fog. I hung in close to some mangrove keys and then along the islands over which the Pinellas Bayway traveled. The road availed auto access for Mullet Key and Fort De Soto County Park, my destination. I drifted into Mullet Key Bayou, aided by a north wind, which brought a chill with it. Whitecaps were foaming by the time I pulled up to the camping area, ditched the boat, and walked to the office to order up a campsite. They told me the campsite charge had gone up by ten bucks! I paid thirty-three dollars for a campsite, the most I had ever paid in my life, and there have been many in the course of writing seven campground guidebooks.

What could I do? The wind was far too strong for me to cross the four-mile-wide Tampa Bay channel, and I'd already been stroking it for hours. And to think I was paying to camp at a place that had once been a quarantine station. Mullet Key had been a few other things before that, though. In the 1840s, a group of U.S. Army engineers visualized Mullet Key as an ideal location to defend Tampa Bay. They procured Mullet Key in the name of the U.S. government, preventing development until a fort was constructed and named Fort De Soto, in 1900. The fort had thick walls and ceilings behind massive mounds of dirt, designed to prevent increasingly powerful artillery from destroying it.

Guns and men were placed in the desolate location. Outbuildings were constructed. Then boredom and misery set in. Biting pests tormented the soldiers. There was simply nothing to do. Lives languished on this lonely key for nine years. The place began being manned by an ever more skeletal crew. During World War I, twenty-six men were left to defend Tampa Bay. By 1923 a single, solitary soul occupied the whole fort. I wonder what he would have done first in case of an attack?

The government tried to sell the fort but couldn't raise a decent bid. Then for a while the state of Florida had a quarantine station here. Are you getting the idea that this place was forsaken? To top it all, during World War II, the government turned Mullet Key into a bombing range.

Finally, Pinellas County got possession of the island chain and developed it as a park. The parks department laid out a design, very well I might add, and the park opened in 1963. In this age of slap-a-condo-everywhere-south-of-Orlando, Mullet Key and the surrounding islands would surely have been built up. But thanks to the army engineers who decided in the 1840s that it looked like a good place for a fort, we have the preserve at Fort De Soto. We must also give some credit to Pinellas County—but do we have to pay such high prices to camp there?

On the positive side, Fort De Soto had a camp store, where I bought a flashlight for a reasonable price. At least they didn't have the most expensive camp store in America. I would be able to see tonight! I spent the brisk and cloudy afternoon inside the campers' day room. Some folks from Quebec had built a fire. They were experienced at that kind of stuff. Other campers shuffled in, warming by the glowing logs. One of the visitors was my next-campsite neighbor. We recognized each other and I waved him over. Robert and I shared an appreciation for the park, it turned out. He made an annual trip from Michigan to Mullet Key. He did some writing as well and promised to drop off a poem he had written about Mullet Key. Here it is:

Medley on Mullet Key

A black-headed gull laughs,
expecting handout at campsite forty-two

A green eye-shadowed egret approaches,
avian panhandler begging for early lunch

Ibises tiptoe gingerly on grass mat,
dining delicately through bent beaks

A fleet of sand crabs scampers for cover
on spongy shore near high tide

Dried brown fronds once chlorophyll green
swing above, dangling swords of Damocles

A squadron of lovebugs swarms over picnic,
flying ineptly, upended by little wind

A noisy whirling wingless bird
crosses diagonally this sunbaked key

Masked bandits under cover of dim light
steal away whole bag of tortilla chips

Troops at nearby Fort De Soto about 1900
fought off mosquitoes rather than munitions

From garrison long empty to campground filled,
the players change but the medley continues

ROBERT J. PALMA

Bob captured Mullet Key in stanza form.

Most tourists from distant places were surprised at the chill this far south. Key West is the only city in Florida that has never recorded a freezing temperature. I spent a restless night listening to the wind power through the campsite palms. Only a fool would go ahead and try to cross Tampa Bay the next day, I thought, but on the other hand, paying thirty-three dollars for a campsite seemed incentive enough to continue.

I made up my mind, then packed rapidly and without hesitation, confirming my decision to cross the bay. I took off into dirty brown waves that contrasted with the steadfast green of the mangrove in Mullet Key Bayou. A gunmetal gray sky portended more bad weather as I paddled hard to cross the ultrashallow yet splashy waters near Bunches Pass. The Gulf pitched and rolled in the distance. Waves crashed with staggering force into a sandbar at the mouth of the pass. I briefly considered turning back but pushed forward over the wave line and was out in the Gulf! To the left some early morning beachcombers walked along Mullet Key. They must have been surprised to see some stupid sea kayaker out there. The waters rolled high and with regularity. I rolled with them. The waves weren't turning over and white capping in the deeper water—yet. My confidence built. I could make it across Tampa Bay—just ride the rollers. I kept forward and soon paddled beyond the south point of Mullet Key. A steady twenty-knot wind, gusting higher at times, came from the northeast and moved me right along. Monster waves were coming in from the open Gulf, which lay to the northwest. I was in the primary shipping lane for Tampa Bay, Egmont Channel, which separated Egmont Key and Mullet Key. As soon as I hit this channel, which ranged in depth from thirty to fifty feet, the water changed dramatically. There were no regular rolling waves here. Suddenly, waves were blasting from everywhere with no readable consistency. It wasn't long before a big one hit me, slamming like an uppercut from a champion prizefighter. My legs nervously quivered as I braced the sides of the Old Town to keep it from turning over. My hands held the metal paddle in a death grip seemingly strong enough to make indentations. Three forces were at work here—the incoming tide, the northeast wind, and incoming Gulf rollers. The deep channel was the final ingredient that conspired to build waves up to seven feet, higher in spots, going in all different directions, pushing, sliding, punching, slapping—coursing wildly. I was in over my head, literally, as I rode this nightmare roller coaster that would make any major theme park ride seem like a child's merry-go-round at a two-bit traveling carnival.

Both ends of the boat were being alternately dipped into the mess and being pushed every which way. It took all my effort to keep afloat, much less keep a steady course south. Even as I diligently watched the waves come from the sides, an occasional rear wave punched me from behind, unexpectedly turning the boat sideways and drenching me to the skin. A channel marker bobbed ahead—it was a six-foot-high metal bell type of channel marker with a light in the middle of it—my southerly guide. A brief glance down at the nautical chart became a chancy and dangerous undertaking. I headed toward the bell and it seemed I might come too close to the beacon—if I hit the bell, the boat and I were history. It was difficult enough keeping upright in this mad hodgepodge of waves, much less avoiding anything. The irony was that this channel marker was the only thing in the bay I could hit! About fifteen feet distant from the bell I rapidly paddled, slicing past the marker with such speed that the bell seemed like a mirage. I had to tuck the paddle in to avoid hitting the bell; the call was that close. My heart beat wildly, accompanied by short, panting, shallow breaths.

The wet, cold metal paddle steadied my quivering arms. This paddle was the only thing keeping me from taking a swim in Tampa Bay, and possibly much worse. At other times the blade had seemed an instrument of torture. Now it was a survival tool. The air temperature was only a little above fifty degrees, but I didn't feel the cold at that moment; my mind was completely consumed with the task at hand as I kept pushing forward.

It might be a good idea to be angling southwesterly toward Egmont Key, I thought. If the boat flipped, at least land would be closer. Egmont Key was a refuge, a national wildlife refuge for brown pelicans, terns, and other nesting birds. Fort Dade was built on Egmont in 1882. Gun batteries were added at the outbreak of the Spanish-American War, and a small community built up around the fort. Old buildings still stand from that community. If the wind blew me into the Gulf beyond Egmont Key, there was no telling what would happen. No other boats of any kind were out, at least in this section of Tampa Bay. Flipping wasn't on the agenda— only a possibility to be thought through. I was grateful for how well the Old Town was handling in the big water and how the spray skirt was taking a major pounding from the water and not failing. I would swim if the spray skirt gave way. Egmont Key was still a good mile away. I managed the kayak over wave after wave after wave. An amazing characteristic of humans is they can get used to anything, from being in prison to being a billionaire. And I was becoming used to this. The deep fear in my gut remained, though the initial shaking and adrenaline rush had subsided. I knew not to let up. As soon as that happened, the waves would flip me over like a pancake at the IHOP.

I just read and then rode wave upon wave. It went like this: get pushed atop the wave, top out, then descend into a trough. Repeat. Get pulled here, then there. Abruptly, a wave picked up the rear of the sea kayak, turning the boat 180 degrees and parallel to an incoming surge that crested above me. Here it came, the swell destined to take me down and push me over. With no time to move I leaned into the rush of green power and dug in the paddle, remembering Tom's suggestion. The salty splash popped my face just as I closed my eyes. In that dark moment of slow motion I began to fall to my left, and dug in farther, grasping the paddle with a death grip. The wave crest passed over me, and then the kayak fell as if in air into a deep trough to my left. I opened my eyes and was still upright, though my hat was off my head, hanging by a string around the front of my neck. My panting shortness of breath and the feeling of impending doom briefly returned. Then I turned the experience around: *If I can survive that wave, I can survive another.*

Anna Maria Island became my goal at this point. Making Egmont Key was a pipe dream. The wind and sea ruled here, pushing me southward. Anna Maria seemed far away, just a flat line of trees with specks for houses. Egmont Key was due west. The waves just kept on, and the fear evolved into a gut ache, like waiting for test results to come back from the lab to see if you have cancer. I passed near another bell channel marker at the south end of Egmont Key and began to feel the effects of the Southwest Channel, another entrance into Tampa Bay. The tide here began pushing me around, though not as wildly as before. The trees and houses of Anna Maria Key were getting closer, slowly but surely, a slow motion relief. I began heavy power paddling—not forcing the paddle though, for there was no forcing my way through the

waves—but rather riding the waves and stroking hard when possible.

Passage Key, just a sandy spit, was ahead. The shallower water
near Passage Key lowered the crazed sea, but the undulations were
still hitting hard, as if the entire force of Tampa Bay was slamming
into me. A look on a map will show that the northeast wind is
exactly the worst kind of wind to have in this spot. Passage Key had
felt the effects of high winds in times past. This sandy spit of thirty
acres had been a wooded mangrove island with a freshwater lake
when the United States established it as a national wildlife refuge
in 1905. In 1920, a hurricane flattened the island, turning it into
the meandering barrier island it is today. Because of its small size
and importance to nesting birds, Passage Key is closed to public
use.

Passage Key looked especially small in the waves, as I paddled
southeast, finally making the shallows of Key Royale Bar. This
sandy shallow at the head of Anna Maria Sound was beaten by
quick, crashing waves turning over the bay floor. I splashed
through the whitewater and the deeper, rolling waters of Anna
Maria Sound—my arms were positively aching and I was chilled
colder than a twelve-pack of beer at a November tailgate before a
Tennessee-Kentucky football game. Paddling slowed the chilling
down toward hypothermia, before I finally stopped in a spot out of
the wind near Cortez. Movies last around two hours, right? This
horror movie lasted about that long too, except it was real. I could
have waited another day at Mullet Key, and in retrospect I probably
should have. But I didn't, and I learned my lesson—two lessons, in
fact. The first was don't cross Tampa Bay in big winds. The second
was don't risk your life for thirty-three dollars.

I was not the first visitor to risk my life in these parts. It was
near Mullet Key that Panfilo de Narvaez entered Tampa Bay in
1527, the first European to have done so. Inspired by the riches
found down Mexico way, Narvaez, along with his cohort Cabeza de

Vaca, sought to uncover the next gold-laden Indian culture. They found an Indian village, discovering a few gold ornaments, and seized the leader, Ucita, to get the information on the source of the gold. Ucita wouldn't reveal its source. Absurdly enough, it appears that the traded gold had come came from Indians who had found a wrecked Spanish ship. Don Quixote may have fought windmills, but these Spaniards were chasing their own gold. Narvaez cut off Ucita's nose. Ucita then made up a story about the great wealth of his enemies, the Apalachee Indians, located south of present-day Tallahassee. Narvaez marched north, sending his ships to Cuba, but he reached the Tallahassee Hills to find only farming villages. The ships returned from Cuba to Tampa Bay but couldn't find the overland travelers, who by this time had returned to the Gulf from inland Florida at St. Marks. Assuming Mexico was only a few days' journey away, Narvaez and de Vaca constructed five long canoes and made it to the Texas coast, where a storm capsized their boats and drowned Narvaez. What remained of this group reached an Indian village where they lived for two years before resuming their slow progress westward and southward. They made Mexico City in 1536. After nine years and six thousand miles, of the group of 280 men who had left Tampa Bay, only four survived, all in the name of gold.

In the nervous morning haste I had made a mistake, not having the next nautical chart ready—the paddle across Tampa Bay had led me off the last chart. When traveling in a sea kayak you must anticipate your daily needs, so as not to be packing, unpacking, and repacking every time you need to get something. I popped the spray skirt loose and got out of the boat, then stood in the water. My numb, wrinkled fingers fished out the nautical chart. I folded up *Tampa Bay and Approaches* and pulled out the new one, *Fort Myers to Tampa Bay*. The Intracoastal Waterway once again became the route. Perhaps some spoil islands lay along the way. Anna Maria Sound pinched in, then I emerged into Big Sarasota Bay, passing Jewfish Key. Named keys are almost always natural islands. The waves were building again here in Big Sarasota Bay, which widened as I paddled southward. A beach lay on the north end of one of the Sister Keys—I aimed the Old Town toward it and glided into the island. A camp lay just onshore—in the maw of the wind blasting forth from the gray clouds above. A better site might be inland. An island exploration revealed an expansive shell mound here, covering several acres and, in places, exceeding ten feet in height. Up on the high ground was a flat shielded from the wind, by Brazilian pepper, of course. This would be my camp. The warmup program began with dry clothes, then a fire, followed by hot coffee. The combination warmed my body and unnumbed my toes.

Now the reality of the foolhardy decision to cross Tampa Bay hit home. *Where would I have been right now if the boat had flipped?* I shuddered at the thought. Would I be on Egmont Key, walking around with no gear or huddled in one of the old buildings there, freezing, wondering what had happened to the boat and all its contents?

Although the weather wasn't currently South Florida–like, the presence of a gumbo-limbo tree on the island heartened me. That said it all. The gumbo-limbo tree is definitely a species of South Florida and points much farther south, here nearing its northern limit. It is more common on the lower peninsula and the Keys. Also known as West Indian birch, gumbo-limbo is nicknamed the tourist tree because of its shiny, peeling copper-red bark. The unusual name is derived from an African phrase meaning "slave's birdlime." Slaves would make sticky glue by boiling the sap of the gumbo-limbo. They would spread the glue on tree limbs to catch birds. Gumbo-limbo sap has also been used for making incense and varnish.

After warming up I decided to do a little repair work—make good use of the time hanging around during the long cold afternoon. I decided to fix the broken bulb on my headlamp. The brilliant idea: take the bulb from the new flashlight and insert it in the broken headlamp. A simple enough plan. I took apart the flashlight and determinedly pulled the bulb fully out of the metal socket housing it. The little wires hanging from the bottom of the bulb after I pulled it out became the new problem. It wasn't going to fit into the headlamp, much less work in the new flashlight any more. Lightless on Three Sisters Key.

I wandered the island; checking out the turtle holes, cacti, and the ever-present Australian pines. The usual amount of sea trash had washed onto land: boards, plastic bottles, beer cans, and natural stuff like seagrass and mangrove driftwood. What did this island look like when the Indians were here? They had eaten all the shellfish upon which I stood. Will the real natural Florida please stand up? I lay on my back, feeling the warmth of the fire, listening to the winds rush through the trees overhead and move water across Big Sarasota Bay. A bald eagle with a fish in its talons perched overhead on a high limb of Australian pine, looking out. The eagle showed it: no matter how unnatural we make a landscape, some elements of nature adapt their instinctual behavior to the new conditions. Florida has more breeding pairs of eagles than any other state in the lower forty-eight. Bald eagles in the South run a little smaller than those up north, but in either case the power curve is the same: the female is larger than the male.

Imagine the terror a fish must experience when it is pulled out of the water alive, into the sky, its flesh being cut by the sharp claws of the eagle. And imagine the eagle, brimming with satisfaction, captured prey in its skilled claws, looking for a perch where it can settle and dine. When the perch is found, the bird tears into the fish with its sharp beak. Certain fear before certain death. There's no room for the ethical treatment of animals here.

I was destined for another 5:00 A.M. awakening, fumbling around in the dark, another dark morning loading the sea kayak without a flashlight. When light came the temperature was about 60 degrees, the fog very dense—I kept a southwesterly course across Big Sarasota Bay, the turquoise water enveloped in a white cloud, like images of an oceanic heaven. There was no land visible; there was never any land. Only the boat, the paddle, and the rolling water existing in a closed world of white nothingness, like those snow globes people pull out at Christmas time. There wasn't even a cormorant. No boats, either. They were fogbound. My Silva compass kept me in a consistent direction, as far as direction went, here in the Sarasota snow globe. A strong following wind pushed the boat and I made the ten or so miles to the south end of Big Sarasota Bay in three hours. The building sun began to melt my foggy world, melting the fog globe. It revealed downtown Sarasota, where there were many residential high-rises. The transition was completed, from darkness to fog and back to stark civilization towering over the turquoise waters. A key difference between the natural world and the human world lies in the shapes and angles used in their construction. The human world uses sharp, abrupt angles—look around; rectangular buildings, square rooms, streets laid out in grids. Now look at nature—trees in rounded-off forms, islands shaped by winds and tides, the curve of a conch shell. Nature flows. The human world is more blunt. And both operate that way.

I paddled through the bay to an agglomeration of more than a hundred sailboats tied up in the water across from the peopled buildings—headquarters of the Sarasota Sailing Squadron, a private club devoted to the time-honored pastime of wind-driven transportation. I was looking to stop, but a sign said "Members Only."

The sun completed its task of clearing the sky. It was now engaged in warming the air. I spotted a beach in the distance and headed for it. The beach was part of a park on South Lido Key near the mouth of Big Sarasota Pass—the primary access into the Gulf here. The Old Town skidded up to the angled sand. I debarked and walked the beach, making for a spigot. The park jumped with anglers and beachcombers. I filled the aqua jug and paddled my way south again, making the twenty-foot-wide canal between Bay Island and Siesta Key. Houses and docks lined the canal. It was an opportunity to see the watery homesites up close—I wouldn't ever have expected this little cut to be the route to the Keys.

The Intracoastal Waterway in Roberts Bay overflowed with boaters. Fathers and sons plied smaller fishing boats. Couples rode inside cabin cruisers, which cut through the water with power and certainty. Sailboats, sails drawn, chugged a little more slowly. There were boats of all kinds, even a sea kayaker or two.

And then there were the fishing boats with flydecks, the tall open decks atop the main deck of the boat, with a separate set of controls up there. For some reason, when a guy gets up in that flydeck he thinks he's a god on water, shoulders erect, head leaning slightly into the wind, sunglasses on, and wind blowing in his hair. He's got the throttle pressed down and is going as fast as possible without regard for other boats. Sixty degrees at forty miles per hour can feel downright chilly. Invariably, on the shielded deck below the flydeck, the boater's companions would have heads hunkered down, backs to the wind, avoiding the chill—no faking like the macho man up top. Roberts Bay eventually narrowed into a No Wake zone accompanied by the usual manatee warning signs along with the Intracoastal Waterway markers.

Everyone but me sped up upon reaching open Little Sarasota Bay. I neared my destination, the Bird Keys. There might be a camp there, but a sign indicated that this was a Sarasota County Marine Preserve. I thought of the Calusas paddling these waters, sign free, in hollowed-out cypress canoes, camping wherever they pleased. The scene had to have been more attractive then. I wished the preserve sign wasn't there, to ease my camping situation. The trouble with signs is that no matter how much you try to ignore them, you cannot look at them without reading them, unless they are in another language or you are illiterate.

Midnight Pass might offer camping nearby. The former Gulf outlet had closed. Hurricanes and other strong natural forces open and close passes between the Gulf and the barrier islands. I paddled to Midnight Pass—now part of the Sarasota County park system, with signs to prove it. There was even a sign with a slash through a tent: no camping. I got out anyway to stretch and passed over a sand dune where boats had once floated. An iridescent green Gulf gently lapped against the shoreline below. It had an amazing appeal and I wished to be out there. However, there were no camping areas along the shore, as houses had gobbled up all available real estate. The Intracoastal Waterway offered the potential for spoil islands, potential camping spots. I explained my dilemma to another visitor. He told me everybody camped on Snake Key, which stood at the mouth of Venice Inlet, a good five or six miles distant. The late afternoon shadows told me to pour on the steam. I did, and soon passed boats left and right. No, just kidding—they were all passing me, as usual, after giving my rig a good stare down. But I stroked the paddle with pride, knowing most of them would never understand the thinking behind my journey. It wasn't about getting from point A to point B but about absorbing what was on the way.

I traversed one more bay, Blackburn Bay, and soon paddled the narrows between Venice and Casey Key. I stopped at a drawbridge and smiled over to some onlookers watching the Sunday afternoon boat parade. The drawbridge then seemingly opened for my passage—giving the few onlookers and me a good laugh. I played to the joke, throwing my shoulders up and acting self-important as I paddled beneath the open drawbridge. Actually, a sailboat with a tall mast waited on the far side, the true cause for the bridge opening. Snake Key was just ahead, lying in the center of the veritable aquatic intersection of Venice Inlet. A marina, houses, a park, and every other sort of beachfront civilization encircled the inlet. It being Sunday, the water lovers were out in droves. Just a few yards away stood another island—the more heavily wooded and secluded Turner Key. I landed the kayak there. A little path led beneath heavy vegetation to a campsite. I achingly heaved the boat out of the inlet up to the island. Soon, darkness drifted over Turner Key and I sat by a little fire, using a cut-open beer can filled with gas and crumpled notebook paper for my nightlight. The lights of the nearby "real" world backlit the camp, shimmering and dancing across the inlet.

I lay on my back, legs bent (they were straight forward in the kayak all day, every day), arms still at my sides, considering the day, which seemed to have lasted a century. I had paddled about twenty-four miles. But what was so bad about that? Our lives pass by so quickly; long days have their merit, especially when you have spent them kayaking. Perhaps this was why I was doing it, to have a long day in the saddle. To feel the ache of a long day was part of the why in why go.

Sounds from across the water drifted onto Turner Key: the clinking of plates and glasses from a restaurant, the laughter of a nighttime volleyball game, cars and motorcycles coming and going, boats idling, the waves crashing into the shore on the Gulf side of the land.

Venice Inlet was much quieter the following morning than twelve hours earlier, but the low hum of Monday morning Venice traffic resonated in the distance. I passed a boat moored to a dock, its stern facing outward. *My Toy,* it said on the back. Why is it that we aquatic travelers always scan the back of a boat, wanting to read its name? And the names are usually so hokey, some cheesy, upbeat "life is great I have boat," phrase: *Getaway, Real Dreams, Bachelor Pad II, My Other Office.* Where are the ones that say "I still owe $60,000 on this boat and feel like I have to use it since I hocked my house to buy it"? I guess there isn't enough space on the back of a boat for that sort of phrase.

I began tracing the Intracoastal Waterway along a man-made canal that connected Venice to Lemon Bay, a long sliver of water lying between Manasota Key and the mainland. The steep-sided, rocked-in Venice Canal headed south. It was a functional connector only; to keep boats from having to head out into the Gulf if traveling south. The canal bore no resemblance whatsoever to the canals in the other Venice, in Italy, but the waterway became much more attractive as it once again neared the Gulf— palms, pines, mangroves. A few bank fishermen stared at rods, then at me—I was the only thing moving and certainly not your average user of the Intracoastal Waterway.

The canal met Alligator Creek and the northern reaches of Lemon Bay. That same strong northwest wind pushed me closer toward the Everglades. Lemon Bay wasn't yet fully developed and had a surprising amount of natural vegetation along the shores. The cynic in me realized that the pine shores, fronted by mangrove, would soon change to docks leading to oversized behemoths pinched together like Baltimore rowhouses. Nearly all privately owned pineland currently left in Florida will be developed. That is a fact. Pineland is high, dry, and the most easily transformed, as opposed to wetlands, which are more protected and where it costs more to prepare the land after the environmental hoops have been jumped through. So when you see a grove of pine trees, imagine a strip mall or housing tract. I can't blame the landowners when somebody throws a small fortune at them for selling their pinewoods. Money talks. And we all want more of it for as many reasons as there are citizens in this country.

I stopped at a marina in Englewood, near Redfish Cove, to buy water. Someone suggested the bait shop. It stank in there. Minnows dying in gurgling tanks, shrimp getting old, and who knows what else decaying. Going to work there must have been a drag for the teenager who manned the bait shop. What a job for a teenager: bait shop boy. They didn't sell bottled water. He offered to fill my jug instead, though he mentioned that "the water here doesn't taste too good." At least Englewood had water, and their aqua beat sea water just the same. Why do we patently trust bottled water and patently mistrust tap water nowadays? When we purchase bottled water, we believe whatever it says on the bottle, thinking some government agency is protecting us from someone putting tap water in a bottle with a pretty label and distributing it. Tap water is more locally controlled, which I am inclined to trust more. I wonder what Englewood will be doing for water a century from now? Desalination is my guess, for Englewood and all of Florida. Invest your money now.

I took lunch before leaving the marina—the usual peanut butter and jelly on flour tortillas. Jelly can have a tough time here in the south end of the state—it doesn't like extended heat. A fungus soon blooms on it in the heat. The jelly's days were numbered. An older fellow walked up as I sat on the pier eating. "You paddling that thing?"

"Yep," I said, answering the obvious.

"I'd like to try something like that, but I'm too old and creaky."

"Nah," I said, trying to make him feel better.

"I wore myself out on the job, working in the steel mills of Gary, Indiana," he replied. I gave him a "So what?" look, not aiming to be mean but wondering what the significance of having worked in a steel mill was.

He went on. "To top it off I commuted to and from Valparaiso for forty-two years. Sixty-mile round trip per day." I nodded, trying to compute the miles, days, and years.

"My son graduated from Indiana University, then got a banking job down here. My wife died a few years back and I followed him."

"How do you like it?" I asked the obviously lonely man.

"Love it. Except the summers are long. I built a small house in Englewood and insulated the hell out of it, but my air conditioning bills are still sky high. It's gotten to where I don't want to get my mail in fear of the electric bill. But what's money? I visit my son and his family, and go back to Indiana twice a year. But all my friends are dying on me. This isn't the way I pictured my retirement."

What do you say to someone whose friends are all dying? I slipped into the cockpit and said, "Good luck with those cooling bills."

"Good luck to you, son," replied the old man as he walked away. I began to paddle. What was the point of dutifully working at a job all your life—to have enough money to live on so that you and your friends could get into a longevity contest? Is the mission or purpose of a life simply to produce offspring to watch them grow and take your place on this earth?

Not the mission, but maybe the purpose. As a thinking man, and a somewhat careful philosopher, I believe the big answers are simple ones. Purpose: Reproduce. Mission: Heaven. Why? We don't really know. But we know that all life "does" is reproduce. Live and die, that is. And we want more, seeking Heaven. And *mon frère*, a rose is a rose by any other name.

Knight Island, farther down the Intracoastal Waterway, is connected to the mainland by a ferry, the only way in or out. The distance between the ferry landing points was about double the length of the boat handling the job. Waterside mangroves shaded the afternoon sun through the Cutoff, which connected Lemon Bay to wide-open Placido Harbor. I drifted under the bridge spanning the gap between the mainland and Gasparilla Island and entered Gasparilla Sound. Just beyond an abandoned low wood and concrete bridge lay an island. I didn't know the name of the island, but a kayaker out for the day had told me about it a few miles back. The island featured high, dry unclaimed land and had a beach landing, meeting my campsite criteria.

After unloading and making camp, I inspected the plot of four acres or so. A torn-up tent flapped in the wind on the west side. Voices from inside drifted in the wind. I neared, wanting to match faces with the voices. The slur of their sounds gave away their day's activities: hitting the sauce. I hollered out a hello and they advised me to come on. The drunken couple in their late thirties talked loudly. The blonde-haired woman, with pigtails that accentuated her wide face, was not as rough looking as she sounded from afar. She sat cross-legged on the tent floor. Her companion lay beneath a scraggly blanket beside her, beer bottle close beside him. His beard partly covered an acne-scarred face. His dishwater blonde locks fluttered in the breeze.

"Y'all know the name of this island?" I asked, after getting through the hellos.

The bearded man sat up and then fell right into telling me an insider's view of how the island came to be named. His soiled windbreaker flapped in the wind as he began. "Some old man used to live on the island, all by hisself. I remember him taking his boat to the marina. He would dock the boat, then walk into this grocery store. I seen him cuz I worked there as a kid. The old man would get his food then I would bag it up. He always insisted on double bags. We were using nothing but paper then. Then he would go back to the boat, load his groceries, and motor to this island. Odd part was, he never said a word to anybody the whole time he was on land. The man must've really liked his solitude. Time went on. I quit the store. Eventually, the old man died and nothing was left on this island but his dogs. Everyone was too scared to go on the island because of the dogs. There was a bunch of 'em and they would go crazy if a boat tried to land. The county finally had to come in and round up the mongrels. Everybody started calling it

Dog Island. Nowadays, people camp here about every weekend—I try to camp here every weekend myself. I ain't staying tonight. You can use my tent and camp here if you want. It's supposed to be windy and cold."

Pigtails nodded emphatically after each sentence then killed her beer at the end of the story. I looked around. They did have a camp here—a lantern, chair, meat smoker, a fire ring, and more blankets in the tent. I wouldn't have gotten under those decrepit blankets unless hypothermia was imminent. But I did borrow their folding chair.

The afternoon light was fading. The couple used the remaining light to jump into their skiff and head back to the mainland. I returned to my own little camp and made supper. Later I made notes and examined the nautical charts, again using the soup can/Coleman fuel light trick. Finally, I slipped into the sleeping bag and lay under the stars, tentless. The upper part of the sleeping bag kept opening in the wind. Brisk air would slide down my back and rouse me. This could have been avoided by facing my feet toward the wind, but once in the bag I was too sleepy to move.

Black morning soon gave way to dawn. I headed south down Gasparilla Sound illuminated by a rising sun. An open blue sky towered over Charlotte Harbor, which widened before me. The lightly choppy water was no immediate hazard, but I was still a little wary crossing Charlotte Harbor, after the Tampa Bay incident. The waves picked up a bit in the open water. A small lighthouse held guard at the south end of Gasparilla Island. Across the harbor was Cayo Costa, an island mostly consisting of a state park, with a few private inholdings. The passage into Charlotte Harbor, cutting between Cayo Costa and Gasparilla Island, was known as Boca Grande. Speedboats were racing through Boca Grande into the Gulf—the winds must be fairly light, otherwise speedboats wouldn't be heading out there. There had been no boats to be seen during the Tampa Bay crossing. Yet another sign I should have

Later I made notes and examined the nautical charts, again using the soup can/ Coleman fuel light trick.

heeded. I had dropped my handy radio—good for weather reports—into the salty sea the day before, quickly retrieving it before it sank, but the water had nevertheless done it in. Salt water is hard on everything.

Cayo Costa is one of the state's finest parks. I had enjoyed many trips here and it was included in my book *Beach and Coastal Camping in Florida*. The park's coastline—sand, buttonwood, mangrove and palm, pine and live oak—resembles what Cuban fishermen saw there a century or more ago. The Cubans used to stop over at Cayo Costa to salt their fish before returning to Havana. There was life before refrigeration. The life of this paddler mirrored that of the Cubans in that sense. All my foodstuffs had to withstand being packed away in a small kayak without preservative cold air, though I could have carried refrigerated items on the Suwannee.

I pulled into the familiar Cayo Costa dock in Pelican Bay. Campers were milling about the morning sunshine, waiting for the ferry to return them to Pine Island and their cars. I stopped for another water run. As usual, sailboats were anchored around Pelican Bay. People with sailboats appreciate the deep bay here, close to the Gulf, yet out of the wind, maybe the very same thing that had appealed to the Cuban fisherman. Back in my own shallow draft boat I passed Useppa Island, another populated enclave accessible only by boat or ferry. Cabbage Key, nearby, was much the same but had a popular overnight getaway, supposedly with good food. I kept south, into Pine Island Sound. The Intracoastal went through here. Boats lined up into a regular parade. The wide-open expanse of the sound allowed me to put a good distance between myself and the motorboaters. That way the paddle became more serene. Those motorboats are so loud! I can't imagine traveling a long distance atop big, loud motors. They killed the atmosphere. Visually, the bay was alluring: sunbeams piercing the translucent seawater, coloring the depths a tropical green. Sugar white sandbars leapt out from the shallows, contrasting with darker waving sea grasses.

Even in such glory I fell into a paddling slump. North Captiva Island and Redfish Pass stayed in the same position relative to the kayak, while the boat parade on the Intracoastal moved toward the far horizon with maddening certainty. My two-packs-of-raisins breakfast wasn't quite cutting it. Supplies were running low and I needed to restock soon. Stroke by stroke I mentally wrestled the paddle. I reached a sandbar, where a quick lunch and a little water revitalized me. I resumed the work (it was nothing but work at this point), running alongside Captiva Island, which was rife with tourists rightly enjoying this gorgeous day—fishing, jet skiing, and lying on the sandy shoreline.

Always aware of the necessity to camp, I didn't think touristy Captiva Island would be a likely spot; a wildlife refuge (no camping) occupied the land that wasn't populated. Nearby Sanibel Island mirrored Captiva with its combination of development and refuge. Where to go? Across the way were more islands. Chino Island lay on the horizon and had tall trees, the harbinger of dry ground. Most of the islands were mangrove, which can mean vast clumps of red mangrove trees intertwined by their unlikely prop roots hanging over mud, not really land at all, unless you happen to be a raccoon. They love these places, prowling the shallows and mud flats for crabs and such. With a decisive turn to the east, I aimed the boat for the green lump dividing sea and sky. Three miles later the detail of Chino Island came into focus. I landed the Old Town on a little sandy break in the mangrove. Dry land rose behind the fringing mangrove—sea grape, buttonwood, and gumbo-limbo trees attested to that. Chino Island would be my camp. Waves battered the small break, and it would be tough getting the gear through the mangrove, so I cruised around the isle looking for a better landing, like the twenty-foot-wide sloping beach I found on the east side.

After making camp in the shade of some Australian pines I followed a trail that led to some rusty machinery and picnic tables shaded by a tin roof. A dock overhung a canal that had been cut into the center of the island. What was the mystery of Chino Island? Stranger still, just off the trail were two raccoon carcasses. They had been skinned and were slowly rotting; that explained the buzzards in the trees. The skinned carcasses gave me a minor case of the creeps. I poked around a little more and spotted a wooden stake bearing the words "Lot 10," spiked into the ground near the canal. A failed development. A passing angler later told me that a land trust had stopped the populating of Chino Island. But what explained the 'coons? And how did the place get the name Chino Island? Had the developer lost his pants?

To name God's creations. How exciting to have bestowed names upon islands, rivers, and bays! I couldn't help wishing I had stepped on this ground first. What would I have named it? What would you name it? Today uncharted or little-charted lands exist in only the most inhospitable places—the ice deserts of Antarctica, the Himalayas, the Andes, the Amazon basin.

Some names are obvious, like that of nearby Pine Island. Pine Island served as a major hub of Calusa Indian life. The Calusa actually built a canal, using slaves captured from other tribes. (Yes, the Calusa kept slaves and weren't quite the noble savages history's revisionists would like you to believe. I like the Calusa myself because they fought the Spaniards tooth and nail, but they lost La Florida just the same.) The Calusa slaves labored with crude digging tools to excavate a canal two and a half miles across Pine Island as a shortcut between Pine Island Sound and Matlacha Pass. The canal averaged twenty feet wide and three to five feet deep. It didn't merely cut across the island at sea level; rather it involved carefully engineered individual segments that incrementally stepped up to the island's thirteen-foot elevation, then back down again. Canal users carried their boats over low dams from each segment to the next.

That evening I once again lay on the ground before a fire. Paddler's body was getting the better of me. I'd say a few Calusa had lain on Chino Island thinking the same thing. The moon moved across the sky between the tree branches faster than I did. I could have been trespassing, lying on manicured St. Augustine grass in someone's front yard, had the land development been realized. I would probably have been looking in at someone watching television, channel clicker in hand, looking for entertainment, staring at a glowing box with rapidly changing pictures. Instead, out here on Chino Island, I made my own pictures, speculating on what might have been, what might yet be, and who had done in the 'coons. Whoever that was now had a couple of good skins. In frontier days, settlers traded 'coon skins, bear skins, deer hides, and more at far-flung trading posts, bartering for powder and lead to get meat and for salt to cure it.

Pine Island Sound lay behind me as I headed easterly, into the morning sun, into an east wind, into San Carlos Bay. Residential high-rises marked Punta Rassa. A trading post had first put Punta Rassa on the map, but it became better known as a cattle port. In the decades after the Civil War and before the railroads came, central state Crackers would slowly drive their cows from the palmetto prairies and plains across the Caloosahatchee River, leisurely herding them seaward, the bovines fattening up on the rich grasses that grew lush after summer storms. These cows were captured wild, using fleet small horses and agile dogs, then branded. Once at Punta Rassa, the cattle were traded for Spanish gold doubloons. As the cattle were loaded onto boats and sent to Cuba, the Crackers, loaded with gold, returned warily to their ranches; robberies were a real possibility. Rough rustlers roamed the prairies, stealing cattle and driving them toward the Ten Thousand Islands, where they too shipped the animals off to Cuba. The life of a Cracker was dangerous. The drives ended when railroads made their way into the heart of the peninsula, whereupon the cattle were herded to railheads and shipped to market.

Modern Punta Rassa could hardly contrast more with those days gone by. A crowded bridge took tourists and workers serving tourists over to Estero Island. A busy marina took other tourists into the Gulf on one of those gambling cruises. I stopped to use the phone and try to snag a campsite at Koreshan, a state park within paddling distance. The park was awfully busy, as I knew from prior inspections of the state's campgrounds. The fellow on the phone told me no campsites were available. I told him I was paddling and couldn't go all over the place in search of a campsite. But fortune was on my side. A cancellation came in while we were on the phone, and he saved the spot for me. Koreshan was not merely a place to lay my head; it is also one of the state's most interesting historic destinations, a must-stop for anyone paddling through Florida history.

I paddled hard past Matanzas Pass into much quieter Estero Bay. A little fancy navigating among mangrove islands minimized a building headwind. The paddle grew heavy near the mouth of the tiny Estero River. Up this river was the Koreshan State Historic Site. Progress transpired slowly as I left the mangrove zone and entered some pineland—almost there. Then came the houses. I had forgotten about the houses, though I had seen them on a previous trip down the Estero River from Koreshan. The state park was farther upriver than I remembered. What looked like a four-hour paddle on the nautical chart had ended up taking eight demoralizing hours. At last the paddle stroking brought me to the park boat landing. I beached the kayak and shambled up a dusty dirt road. The sun bore down overhead. By the time I reached the paved road and followed it to the sun-blazed park headquarters I was certifiably whipped, besides being covered in saltwater film.

A park ranger of around my age got me a campsite. I recognized his voice—the fellow I had spoken to on the phone. He could read the exhaustion on my face and offered to tote my gear from the landing to my campsite. I took him up on it. Mike and I hit it off right away. Beneath his blond hair and sky blue eyes was a man satisfied with his work. Once a stressed-out banker, Mike had come to Koreshan to camp, getting away. He liked the place so much that the next thing he knew, he was working at the state park, leaving behind good money but also the go-go-go of his former job. Being a ranger was a still a job, but he described it as helping other campers reduce their stress level from the rigors of their jobs, just as he had first enjoyed at this haven. I could relate; that's about what an outdoor guidebook writer does too.

Koreshan was a haven of sorts in times past, and this is part of the story of how it came to be a state park. A man went to Florida with a vision of a new community based on a religion he started after having an "illumination." Following his illumination, Dr. Cyrus Teed renamed himself Koresh (Hebrew for Cyrus) and founded a new version of Christianity based on communal living, celibacy, and a universe inside the earth. Also, Koresh taught his followers he was immortal. Koresh/Teed had already made two attempts to establish communities up in New York, then made it to Chicago, where his ideas took hold. But Chicago wasn't the place for Koresh; he wanted to build a "New Jerusalem," a city of ten million people all living under the tenets of his faith. He made his way down to Florida and boated up the Estero River, led by a fellow named Damkohler, who had a farm upstream. Teed worked his magic on the German, who donated the land for the project.

The part about the universe inside the earth was called "Cellular Cosmogony," which Koresh "discovered" in 1870. In Koresh's world, the universe was actually concave, curving at eight inches per mile, according to his calculations, and humans lived inside a hollow sphere. This universe fell within the capability of human comprehension, unlike a universe without end. His followers reached the Estero River in 1894 to form a community where they practiced what Teed preached.

Teed made his stab for the ideal in his Koreshan Unity, an offshoot of Christianity. Each member of the sect worked for the good of all. Both traditional and vocational education were stressed, as was Koreshan Cosmogony and how the world worked according to Koresh. Members were offered a secure, insulated life, to open an era when New Jerusalem would eventually expand to include millions of people in this planned city. What you see in the park, the Home Grounds, is about as big as it got. There were some nearby offshoots such as on Mound Key. Turning the wilderness into a settlement amounted to a lot of hard work, a tenet of the Koreshans, but there weren't enough other converts, despite Teed's traveling and lecturing wherever he could.

The group became self-sufficient and sold their excess products, including bread and some finished goods, to outsiders. They continued working on building the community until Teed died in

1908. Thinking he would be resurrected, members refused to bury their leader until the Lee County coroner forced them to do so. The Koreshans placed him in a tomb, which was destroyed in the 1921 Hurricane. Oddly enough, the body of Cyrus Teed, a.k.a. Koresh, was never recovered.

After his lack of immortality was exposed, the sect began to dwindle. Some members carried on; some drifted away. Without Teed, the surviving members found recruiting new Koreshans difficult, and the celibacy policy of the cult got in the way of reproducing new members. As the group aged, the Koreshans saw the end. In 1961 the final four members donated the land and buildings to the state in Teed's memory. The last Koreshan to live at the settlement, Mrs. Hedwig Michel, is buried on the grounds. But Teed is getting one of his wishes, that of a city of ten million people in southwest Florida. The Koreshan settlement, once in the back of beyond, is now a preserved haven in a sea of shopping malls, car dealerships, row upon row of houses, and traffic on U.S. Highway 41 that rivals the crush anywhere in Florida.

That night, in the campground near the buildings of the Koreshan Unity, I slept like the dead. I decided to lay over for a couple of days, taking care of small details and resting my paddling muscles. The grounds of the settlement offered a glimpse into the past. Damkohler's house stands near the river. The Founder's House, where Koresh lived, is the oldest Koreshan-built structure, finished in 1909. There are also sunken gardens, a bakery, residential cottages, and a machine shop. The Art Hall functioned as the center of cultural, social, educational, and religious activities. A look inside shows a picture of what Teed envisioned New Jerusalem would be like.

The next couple of days were warm and sunny, nearing idyllic. There were many friendly campers at Koreshan, including a chain-smoking artist from Minnesota whom I'd met on previous trips. Koresh would have been a good place to stay for a long while, but I had a journey to continue, heading south, to reach the Everglades. The Sunday morning of my departure dawned foggy. I went to a park program where campers and park volunteers met for coffee and doughnuts. It was a pleasant way to say good-bye. The day was warming as I hauled my gear to the boat landing. The trail cut beneath the fragrant pine woods of the picnic area to reach the Estero, my river of return to the sea.

An outgoing tide pushed me out on a paddle much more pleasant than the one up the river. I was well rested. Soon Estero Bay lay spread beneath a bright sun, glimmering among the islands of green. I aimed the boat for Mound Key, a state historic area in Estero Bay. I took the trail from a shell landing and explored the island. Southwest Florida has the greatest concentration of Indian shellwork sites in the United States. This is not surprising, considering the abundance of marine foods and the vast amount of coastline. Mound Key was home to Calusa from around 100 to 1750 A.D. As I've already noted, in their daily lives they discarded food shells, fish bones, broken tools, and pots, forming piles of garbage. These Indian middens were recycled by the Calusa, being used to form mounds, terraces, and platforms. The very ease with which they obtained food left time for building structures and developing a more complex society, hence the establishment of village centers like Mound Key. When Spaniards arrived on the southwest Florida coast in the 1500s, they brought missionaries with them, establishing a fort and mission at the capital city of the Calusa, known as Calos. According to mission records, this capital held around a thousand people and was located on an island in the middle of a bay, two days' sail from Havana. Only two islands, Mound Key and Useppa Island, fit this description and are large enough to contain so many people. Spanish artifacts from the 1500s have been found on Mound Key, leading many people to conclude that Mound Key was the Calusa capital. It is hard to look at this island today and see

a thousand residents. It's even harder today to believe that somewhere in the state actually lost population.

The tide was filling Estero Bay as I picked up a marked channel
leading toward the town of Bonita Springs. The town was busy
joining the tourist circuit. Monstrous cranes towered over half-
built high-rises. Bonita Springs, just north of Naples, wasn't going
to let the tourist dollars whistle right on by to Naples. The tourists
were out in force, piloting pontoon rental boats to enjoy the pretty
day. Emblazoned on the sides of the boats in lettering a foot high
or more were signs shouting out: "Estero Bay Boat Rentals, (941)
525-2264" and "Rent Me for Only $120 per Day." Everyone who
looked at those boaters knew they were tourists. Of course, most of
the people looking at them were other tourists, also in rental boats.
Perhaps they compared rates.

I paddled into Little Hickory Bay. The marked channel narrowed. Ahead stood an island unlike the other low-slung mangrove isles—the Australian pines showed it. The Sunday afternoon boat parade passed directly by the unnamed patch of land,
but I knew that camping opportunities were limited ahead. Naples
and the high-rise hotels wouldn't favor having a sea kayaker over-
nighting on their beach, especially after what the hotels paid for
that beachfront.

I beached the Old Town on the island. Beyond the sandy landing, just a narrow cut between mangroves, stood high ground
sporting mainly Australian pines and the ever-present Brazilian
pepper. A few native species were clinging on for life, including
Jamaica dogwood. The modest little island was a veritable United
Nations.

I pulled the boat out of the water and up to the campsite, then
relaxed in the shade, surprised at the first really hot day of the trip.
No bugs, though. Lizards skittered through the leaf litter. Lizards
typically have dry scaly, skin, clawed feet, and external ear open-

ings, as opposed to amphibians like salamanders and frogs. Most Florida amphibians are nocturnal, whereas lizards also are active by day, even in the midday heat. Near the camp, as on many other shell mounds, was a steep-sided hole, evidence of some excavation by an artifact hunter. I started out on top of the sleeping bag that night, pulling the bag over my body only later once the air cooled down. This would be the last night of sleeping out in the open, as the bugs would start buzzing south of here.

Another sunrise colored the boat near Wiggins Pass. I had left before the sun rose and I needed the flashlight to see the nautical chart. Serenity flooded the waters, free of the combustion engine. Other sounds enhanced the morning. I listened to pelicans fly overhead, actually hearing wings flap as they returned to the Gulf. I could hear the waves crashing on the far side of Wiggins Island. Let me be clear: I appreciate a combustion engine and how it helps me get around, but I also appreciate the sounds of nature without a four-stroke rumbling in my ear.

Brown pelicans are birds nearly everyone can identify. These large stocky birds have a long flat bill with a pouch under it. They are seen along beaches and lagoons in the wild, or on pilings and around docks, looking for handouts. When fending for themselves they fly over the water, plunging in, then resurfacing to swallow their catch. At docks, they wait for the boats to come in, so that they can enjoy the leftovers when anglers are cleaning fish.

The short Cocohatchee River flowed as a mostly tidal waterway. And the tide poured out that morning in full force. The Cocohatchee shot me through Wiggins Pass into the Gulf like a cannon. Beyond the force of the river, the Gulf spread as flat as the lanes at my favorite bowling alley. I headed south. Beachcombers were plying the shores of Delnor–Wiggins Pass State Recreation Area, a tiny parcel of natural beach just north of the high-rises, to the north of Naples. The buildings were up there—twenty, thirty, and forty stories high, looming above the low-slung shore where many

I pulled the boat out of the water and up to the campsite, then relaxed in the shade, surprised at the first really hot day of the trip.

a Calusa Indian had once paddled past. Whatever would they think now?

A fog drifted amid the line of hotels, cooling the morning. The Naples City Pier loomed ahead. Folks tossed in lines from this Gulf-side venue. With so many anglers with so many lines so close together, it seemed they must get hung up together. The rest of the town of Naples felt more subdued after the marching column of high-rises side by side. Here were a lot of well-landscaped houses and drainage pipes leading from the mainland to the sand shore. Many pipes were covered with rocks, as if that would make them look less unlovely.

A plethora of boaters were out. It seemed they were getting back at me for enjoying the solitude of the early morning. Naples would

The buildings were up there—twenty, thirty, and forty stories high, looming above the low-slung shore where many a Calusa Indian had once paddled past. Whatever would they think now?

be behind me if I could only get across Gordon Pass, which connects Naples with the Gulf. Speedboats, sailboats, and cabin cruisers blocked my path. Finally I took my shot and paddled like mad, bouncing in the multitude of wakes.

By the time I reached Keewaydin Island, a barrier island south of Gordon Pass, the fog had long burned off. A white sun beamed down on the blue water. Afternoon shellers hunted across the bright sand of the island. Keewaydin seemed natural, with sea grape, mangrove, and coconut palm, and a few Jamaica dogwood and gumbo-limbo trees. Although common down this way, coconut palms are not native to the state. This tropical import is used in landscaping around dwellings and roadsides. The swaying trunk of the coconut palm is a symbol of warm and sunny South Florida. The coconut palm is an exceedingly useful tree. Its fruits can be eaten raw and the inner liquid is good to drink. The dried, oily parts of the fruit are used in making soap and coconut oil. The leaves are used as thatch for roofing and the trunks for posts in structures. Coconut shells are used as bowls, and the tree fibers have been made into mats, ropes, and brushes. Perhaps this is why cartoonists routinely drawn in a coconut palm when their victims are stranded on islands. Coconuts might indeed keep a castaway alive.

A bright yellow tent dominated the shoreline ahead. A sunbather, smeared in grease and brown as mahogany, lay in a lounge chair. The yellow tent was his. I hollered to inquire whether he knew who owned the island. Mr. Mahogany was from Jersey, his accent as strong as salt spray in your eyes. I could barely understand the fellow. Gradually I deciphered that he wasn't sure who owned the island, but he had been camping here for years, for free. I paddled toward the south end of the island, seeing another group of campers, then found my own camp, in the shade. After being in the sun, and on the water, which reflected the sun, and nearly continually heading south, my eyes and body were ready for a break from old Sol.

After being in the sun, and on the water, which reflected the sun, and nearly continually heading south, my eyes and body were ready for a break from old Sol.

In the shade of sea grape trees, I checked out the maps and nautical charts, examining places already seen and places yet to go. Then I took a little walk along the beach. The sand was littered with shells—fighting conchs, most with their orange-brown shells partly broken, lay alongside turkey wings. Narrow pen shells; a small white cone-shaped Florida cerith; oyster shells. Area beaches like Cayo Costa and Sanibel Island are known for their shelling. This was undoubtedly a lesser-known sheller's beach. Black-bottomed clouds had built over the land and were threatening westward but couldn't seem to make it over the Gulf. They did make it to the beach, dropping rain while I was a mile or more from camp. I ran back in a sweat as the rain pelted the beach. Upon reaching camp, I erected the tent, which made the rain stop. Of course, putting up the tent doesn't always stop the rain.

The boats had mostly left by sunset. Quiet returned. The lights of Marco Island twinkled in the distance. Rhythmic waves lulled me into slumber land, aided by a pitter-patter of showers during the night. Night herons flew over with their trademark "quawk."

By morning the rain had refreshed the air—and wet everything, too. I put the soggy tent into a dry bag, wondering about the point of putting something wet into dry storage. I headed south again along Keewaydin Island. Since 1952, this barrier island has migrated a mile and a half southward, causing Little Marco Island to lose most of its beachfront. Barrier islands tend to drift, both from the effects of day-to-day wind, waves, and tidal action and when there are cataclysmic hurricanes. Barrier islands are formed three ways: when a spit from the mainland is breached by an inlet; when a portion of a dune line is stranded by rising water levels; and through the emergence of underwater shoals. When homeowners build on these barrier islands, there is a real possibility of the land they have bought literally washing away. The houses on the south end of Keewaydin are in fairly good shape, since barrier islands south of Tampa Bay have a southward drift. Don't build a house on the north end of these barriers islands—your land might disappear under you.

I paddled on the Keewaydin Island extension toward where I'd seen lights the night before, Marco Island. The island had lost its twinkle. It was just another row of tall towers, laid out in a half arc. Tigertail Beach fringed its north end. Tourists were walking the beach, looking for shells, and riding jet skis. Parasailers rode high in the sky at the end of a rope attached to a boat. Can you imagine what the inventors of this pastime went through perfecting their craft?

Marco Island was another important Calusa habitation and is the site of one the state's most interesting archeological finds. In 1896, Frank Cushing found wooden and fiber artifacts preserved in the coastal muck among platforms, terraces, and canals similar to those on Mound Key. Normally, pottery and shell items are found at Calusa sites. But in this preservative mud were throwing sticks for spears, wooden bowls and war clubs, a canoe paddle made from cypress, buttonwood and gumbo-limbo trees, and fiber nets with the floats still attached. But the most striking were wooden masks, faces with eyes, ears, and mouths. Most of the masks, averaging twenty inches in height, had an animal theme. Unfortunately, when the painted masks were taken from the muck, they dried and disintegrated, though Cushing managed to save some of them.

The big buildings ended at Marco Island. I turned the Old Town east, into Coxambas Bay, into the fabled Ten Thousand Islands. The Ten Thousand Islands are a profusion of mangrove isles, ranging from hundreds of acres to a single tree forming the smallest of islets. Most of the named islands are called keys, from the Spanish for island. It was here in Coxambas Pass, among the dunes, that freshwater springs had sated the thirst of the Calusa of

Marco Island and pirates and Cuban fishermen had filled their water casks. Coxambas is derived from the Spanish word *cacimba*, the "place of wells."

A warm wind blew from the east, the direction I headed, pushing through a mangrove-flanked channel between Horse Island and Helen Key. While running directly alongside the mangrove I startled an osprey busy trying to eat the fish in its talons. A fishing osprey is quite a sight, diving steeply into the water, talons outstretched, pulling out a fish, and adjusting the fish in its claws so that the prey's head points forward as the bird flies off. Pesticide use almost did in the osprey during the 1960s, but it has come back strongly along the Florida coast, where it is widespread. Ospreys often let you know when you pass a little too close, giving sharp calls of irritation.

The expanse of Gullivan Bay stretched out beyond Helen Key. The miles-wide bay showed little wind. Gulf-facing beaches fronted many of the keys. Most islands are federally owned, part of the Ten Thousand Island National Wildlife Refuge. The rules at this refuge allow camping, so it was only a matter of finding the right site.

Clouds had built over the mainland and were drifting west but would lose their steam over the Gulf. What was happening was this: in the morning, the sun comes up and warms the earth. Air warms more quickly over land than over the water. This creates a temperature difference between land and water, kicking up that daily breeze. As the air rises, it encounters lower air pressure higher in the atmosphere and expands. This expansion causes the air to cool, which causes the moisture in the air to condense and form clouds over land. In winter, the clouds usually aren't dense enough to bring rain like they do in summer, but they form over land and then dissipate when they reach the sea, because the air over the water isn't as warm. The air over the water doesn't rise, expand, cool, and condense at the same rate as the air does over the land. Therefore, someone traveling along the coast will see clouds over the land and not over the water.

I paddled east over four miles of open water, the sun warming my back, and reached Gullivan Key for a stop. Sea grape and mangrove lined the beach. I kept on; the day was made for paddling, so I aimed for Panther Key. This alluring island features a long beach, also fronted by sea grape, buttonwood, and some sea oats on the north end. Under the whim of the tides a small creek flowed in and out of the heart of the island. Sea oats are an important land builder on barrier islands, so important that Florida law protects the plant. Its seeds are blown onto beaches, where the plant begins to root into the sand, stabilizing the beach. Lateral growth helps build sand dunes. Dunes are constantly being built up and torn down as storms or high tides cover the sea oats. Dry blowing sand can bury the plants, and they must start the colonization process over again.

I arrived around high tide and quickly unloaded the boat, getting the chores over before my customary post-paddling stretch. The beach begged a walk. I crunched over the sand, noting the plastic poles on the perimeter between sand and vegetation, marking sea turtle nesting sites. Sometime between May and September, female turtles crawl onto the upper part of a beach and each deposit about 120 eggs into holes dug with their hind flippers. A female may do this several times during a nesting season. From this point, the eggs face overwhelming odds; only one egg per nest will likely survive to adulthood. The threats begin while they are still beneath the sand. Raccoons and shorebirds feed on the eggs. After this, the hatchlings must evade fish. But these long odds have been taken into account in the sea turtles' reproductive habits over time. What hasn't been taken into account are the loss of beaches from seawalls and bulkheads, losses to human poachers, and the way artificial lights confuse hatchlings, making them wander inland instead of to the sea. Ten Thousand Islands National

Wildlife Refuge is important for sea turtles, and they are a subject of study here.

To the east lay another refuge, except it was termed a reservation. It was for human beings, Miccosukee and Seminole. Growing up in Tennessee, I never had much of a concept of an Indian reservation. All the Indians had been pretty much pushed into Oklahoma, and I had never seen one except in school books. That word *reservation* always puzzled me. Could you leave a reservation? Or was it like a big jail? It sounded as if the Indians must make it or die there; as if they couldn't leave or interact with those outside the reservation. It might be called a preservation, where people could try to preserve portions of their traditional way of life after being flung into the modern world by default.

The dilemma of how to preserve the past for the future remains. Indians have relinquished the subsistence culture of obtaining food, clothing, and shelter from their surroundings, but many face another kind of subsistence living: living in a battered trailer and waiting for a government check. The struggle to preserve traditional lifeways yet adapt to modern ones is a time warp spanned by the precarious bridge of two cultures merging. Indians don't wear much leather any more. Generation by generation, fewer people speak the old tongues. Casinos have brought money to some tribes, reducing the poverty. But casinos in the Everglades? This would be the complete opposite of the spirit of the River of Grass: total artificiality designed to exploit human weakness. Excitement, lights, whistles, bells, and music bombarding you. Masses of people stampeding into group madness, directed, cared for, entertained, and drained while sliding from the slot stool to the buffet line. And you don't have to do anything except open your wallet. Do Indians take the interstate to the modern world and take advantage of what it has to offer, or do they reject the whole gig and preserve their cultural heritage?

Walking along a deserted beach is a great time to think, I thought, while sweatily returning to camp in a dying sunset.

Walking along a deserted beach is a great time to think, I thought, while sweatily returning to camp in a dying sunset. The temperature neared 85 degrees. I leaned against a buttonwood, intending to prepare supper, but the no-see-ums put a stop to that. They controlled the dusk. So I retired to the tent, which functioned more like a sweat lodge. It took a good thirty minutes to cool down in there. Meanwhile, the crickets came on duty, serenading from the mangroves, while I watched the world lose its color, changing to black and white, mostly black. Marco Island shone again, just a white haze over the trees, this time to the north.

I finally got out and tested the air. The no-see-ums had thinned. I wonder where they go at night? There always seem to be fewer of them when it's dark. Another bland supper bubbled in the pot, but the ambiance couldn't have been matched at your favorite five-star eatery. The sky hung so heavy with stars that I feared they might fall down on me. I sat on the kayak, at the beach, massaged by a gentle sea breeze. Waves lapped at the shore, serenading my table with music that would put the most talented restaurant pianist out of work.

A late moon aided an early morning start, and I paddled the Ten Thousand Islands by moonlight, staying on the "outside," as the Gulf is known to Everglades paddlers, until full light. I passed Camp LuLu Key, a privately owned island, then soon hit Indian Key Pass. It led to Everglades City and the Gulf Coast Ranger Station. The early morning cruise turned into hard work in Indian Key Pass, as the tide poured out full bore from Chokoloskee Bay. An east wind backed the tide. I had the double whammy against me and had to work for every foot. These things happen. Sometimes the wind blows your way, sometimes it doesn't; same with the tides. Chokoloskee Bay chopped erratically, and I beat directly across it, arriving at the ranger station by noon. Friends were in there.

I changed out of my wet, sea-soaked duds into clean ones—a slight improvement, though this didn't get the scruff off my face or make me smell much better. I went in to visit Judy Hayes, an ex-Tennessean. She loved South Florida. Judy had helped me when I was writing an Everglades paddling guide. I got a campsite across the street at the Glades Haven campground and walked my stuff there from the boat launch, being fried by the sun. Once I had cleaned up, Judy let me borrow her car and I went to the grocery store, replenishing my supplies. It was a good thing the speed limit was thirty on the main drag of Everglades City, since I topped out at twenty—this was the first time I had driven a car in six weeks, and a borrowed one at that.

In the evening I sat at my campsite picnic table, reading the biannual Everglades newspaper. A fresh wind blew from the interior Glades. A miniature city of trailers and campers surrounded me, lit by numerous street lamps. The atmosphere contrasted mightily with that at Panther Key the night before. It was taking the adventure out of this adventure. Music blared from a nearby trailer. One of its occupants moseyed my way, en route to the laundry room. He asked what I was reading. I told him. He asked what I was doing down here. I told him. Then I turned the tables, asking about him. He lit a cigarette, put one foot on the picnic table, and said, "I'm a crabber."

"Tell me more," I inquired.

"Okay, but let me put these clothes in the wash first." He returned, sat down, then lit another cigarette. "Crabbing is pretty good. I get off work at 3:30 and make from 125 to 175 bucks a day. We get up at 4:30. I'm on the boat by 5:30, and then we head nine miles out, checking trap lines. I stand in the front of the boat, the bow, pulling traps, pulling crabs out, real quick, before they bite me, then bait the trap, and throw it all back in the water, like clockwork, before the next trap comes." He was talking about stone crabs. Everglades City claimed to be the stone crab capital of the United States. "After running the lines we pull claws, only the legal ones. The state sets a certain length, ones we're not sure of we throw in a doubter box, and figure them out later, a little slower. Then we head back in, hose our slickers off, then clean the boat. My captain's a bitch; he wants a very clean boat. I really don't like that one thing— cleaning that boat. Then we're done."

"Then what?" I asked.

He sucked on the cigarette. "We finish. Maybe we drink a few beers, maybe we don't. I get paid cash every day. My boss pays for the trailer in the campground. I own a house in Naples." I doubted that. "When I get enough money," he went on, "I'm gonna get back in construction, though. I'll buy some tools with some of this crab money. There's so much work in Naples." I believed that, after seeing all the construction.

"The fishing's dying around here anyway," he said. Wade was his name. "The commercial fishing, that is. All the Yankees are coming down here, moving down here, buying property and building tourist places, high-rises and all that is needed to serve them. All that oceanfront is going. What do they do when they get here? One thing is fish—with rod and reel. That's why the state passed the constitutional amendment on the net ban—netting looks bad." He was referring to the ban on using a net for catching mullet, which is an important bait fish on which game fish feed. Rod and reel anglers seek the game fish. Some people thought the netting of mullet deprived game fish of food.

"So they come down, buy our land, change our laws, so they can sport fish. The result, local fishermen can't net mullet, which brought in money, and the cost of bait to put in traps—mullet—rises. Then the cost of gas rises, so fishermen can't operate boats. And we can't afford a place to live, since land values have shot out of sight with the Yankees puttin' up resorts. There's hardly a fisherman left in Naples. The same thing is happening here. A development is going up right now, a mile away, on the Barron River. Then developers will buy more land to build businesses to serve the Yankees in those hotels. The fishermen, native Floridians who have been here for generations, are squeezed out, just like what happened in Naples. And the hilarious thing is this—those tourists will be expecting fresh fish and crabs and there won't be anybody to provide it for them, just like us fishermen won't be able to provide for our families."

Wade was right. Everglades City was going, going, gone, like Naples, Marco Island, and nearby Goodland, from fishing village to snowbird haven. I was seeing a snapshot of Florida at the turn of the new millennium, a Florida much changed and now changing even faster.

A hundred years ago there was enough land along the banks of the Allen River (later to become Barron River) for a couple of families to settle. In the 1920s Barron Collier swung behind the development of a road connecting the east and west coasts of lower Florida, linking Tampa and Miami. He set about acquiring 90 percent of southern Lee County, later to become Collier County. He needed a base of operations for the road, dubbed the Tamiami Trail by a witty Miami editorialist. A dredge scooped up spoil from the waters around the Allen River. Available land for Everglades City rose from 100 to 660 acres. A town sprang up for the construction workers, who completed the Tamiami Trail in 1928. Residents turned to fishing, and for a while things stayed that way, slowly feeling impacts from increased tourism and the establishment of Everglades National Park. Now the pace is accelerating.

Is change good, bad, or indifferent? Wade fried some fresh fish and I ate with him and his roommate Sam, another native Floridian. Sam realized the prognosis but resisted it, including the state-funded job training for displaced fisherman. He was a fisherman, like his father, and he intended to ride the last fishing boat into the sunset.

7　Everglades National Park

I slept until light for the first time in a long time, although this was among the least wild of all my campsites. Here my slumber was threatened not by wild animals but by those very bright street lamps that had been my reading light. I walked across the road and the lawn back to the ranger station and obtained an Everglades National Park backcountry camping permit. It laid out my itinerary for traversing the park. Inside the visitor center, I reveled at the various languages spoken. Foreigners. Lots of foreigners. My star-spangled heart was proud that they would travel so far to see the natural beauty of the United States. That led me to wondering where all the Americans were. Technology has brought a world where we can see everything on a forty-inch color screen or a nine-teen-inch monitor. Why actually visit the Everglades when you can see a one-hour video of the park from your favorite chair? Who needs reality when we have virtual reality? On the other hand, look at the Smoky Mountains National Park. It is suffering from overappreciation. I like to contemplate people appreciating nature, but overappreciation can be a problem. Catch-22.

When I returned to the campground a couple of fellow paddlers engaged me in conversation, and I asked them for a ride to carry my stuff over to the put-in behind the ranger station. Pam and Tom were from Kitty Hawk, North Carolina, and were fixing to take a college group into the Everglades. Paddlers unite. Finally, I hit the water about 1:00 P.M., stroking the blade into a steady headwind, crossing Chokoloskee Bay on the famous Wilderness Waterway, a marked ninety-nine-mile route through the Everglades, connecting Everglades City with Flamingo in the southern reaches. Ahead lay Chokoloskee Island, a massive shell mound of some six hundred acres, long occupied by humanity. In the late 1800s plume, hide, and fur hunters came, followed by families living in much the same way as the Seminoles, getting what they could from the sea and growing a few vegetables on the side. In 1906, Ted Smallwood established a trading post, buying hides, furs, and produce, like tomatoes grown on nearby Sandfly Island, and selling goods unavailable in the wilderness. Civilization crept up on Chokoloskee when a causeway linked it to the mainland. Smallwood's store remained open until 1982. It has since been reopened as a museum, capturing the Ten Thousand Islands of times past. I paddled by the dock to the old store.

The most notable incident to have occurred on Chokoloskee Island was the slaying of Ed Watson. He had come to the Everglades in the 1890s with a troubled past. Rumor had it that he had killed the famous Belle Starr, and a few others, before settling about three miles inland from the Gulf on the Chatham River, a few miles south of Chokoloskee. He built a two-story house along the river, near his thriving cane and vegetable farm of thirty-five acres atop on an old Indian shell mound. Neighbors kept an eye on Watson. Other ruffians and drifters joined him from time to time, working on his farm. In 1910, some of Watson's workers were seen in the Chatham River—floating with weights attached to their gutted bodies. Word spread and the ire of nearby Chokoloskee Island rose to fever pitch. Watson was away, and he stopped at Chokoloskee on his return from Marco Island. When he landed, someone asked Watson for his gun. He refused and was shot too many times to count by the armed men. They towed his body by boat to nearby Rabbit Key and buried him. He was later reburied near Fort Myers, where his deceased wife already lay.

Watson's farm, now part of Everglades National Park, was known as Chatham Bend. Today the cleared area is less than one acre, but you can see the remains of a syrup kettle, a cistern, and farm implements of his time. Others lived there after him. Eventually, the house burned down. Some of the trees Watson planted still stand. Determined explorers can venture through the thickets near the homesite to see more relics of his operation. Be forewarned: the bodies of several Watson victims were never found . . .

The rising tide helped me get the sea kayak through the shallow south end of Chokoloskee Bay. Lopez River lay ahead. The tide ran up the river but was negated by the wind. The double-bladed paddle was the only thing that was going to get me anywhere. Soon enough the Old Town was scraping up to the shell bank of the Lopez backcountry campsite. It was another Calusa shell mound and later the home of early Everglades homesteader Gregorio Lopez. Lopez came to the Everglades from Spain in the 1890s. The remnants of a large water cistern lie right on the bank of the river, inscribed "1892" on the side facing the river. People collected rainwater in such cisterns for their daily use. There are two seasons down here, rainy and dry. The rainy season extends from late April through November. After this, rainfall is unreliable, so Lopez and other Glades settlers would build sizable cisterns to store enough water to last through the dry season. The Lopez River flowed brackish, undrinkable.

The boat landing at Lopez campsite is actually part of the shell mound that extends into the river. Mangrove fronts the camp. The ground here is high and dry. I found a shady tent site beneath a large buttonwood and a few gumbo-limbo trees, upriver of the cistern. A tall tamarind tree hung over the water. The scene was noiseless, save for lizards skittering about in the dry leaves on the campsite floor. Then I heard a collective *whoosh, whoosh, whoosh.* Overhead a flock of ibis flew by, their black-tipped wings contrasting against the blue sky, broken by friendly clouds.

The Lopez River was my flowing companion that night, as sweet air drifted downriver. Occasional swishes and jumps in the water signaled the game of chase below the surface. A porpoise rose for air. A shooting star blazed across the night sky. What a thrill to be *in* the Everglades.

A steady tide pushed me up the Wilderness Waterway the next morning, up Crooked Creek, just beyond the Lopez River. A brawny morning sun penetrated the cool morning air. The Wilderness Waterway pushed into a series of bays connected by small creeks. On I paddled, through Sunday Bay, Oyster Bay, Huston Bay, Last Huston Bay, then Chevelier Bay. These open expanses of water, a mile or two across, were ringed in mangrove and just a few feet deep. I felt like a well-tuned paddling machine, slipping across the water in an ideal interaction of blade, body, and boat. The nautical chart below me barely received a glance in these familiar waters.

A high-pressure cell off the Atlantic kicked up the southeast winds again. It was the Bermuda high, which parks off the Florida east coast in winter, keeping the clouds from collecting moisture and building to culminate in an afternoon thunderstorm. Otherwise the rainy season would last all year long. The wind blew across the bay in fits, upsetting the still water, the invisible wave speeding toward me and I toward it. Beyond Chevelier Bay, I drifted into Darwins Place backcountry campsite for lunch. This high ground, located on Possum Key, is a popular backcountry campsite for motorboaters. Darwins Place is located atop an old Calusa Indian mound beside a small creek connecting Chevelier and Cannon bays. Jean Chevelier settled on Possum Key in the 1880s, working as a plume hunter and collecting bird specimens for museums—working both sides of the fence, if you will. Chevelier died in 1895. By that time, Lige Carey had built a house here. A string of others, including the Cannon of Cannon Bay, called Possum Key home. The last man here, Arthur Leslie Darwin, was also the last private citizen to live in Everglades National Park. He moved to Possum Key in 1945 and grew bananas to sell, living out his days on the island. You can still see the outline of his concrete house. Possum Key was much more open in Darwin's day; it has grown over since his death after thirty years there. However, the park service has cleared the mound somewhat, cutting back the Brazilian pepper and leaving fig, gumbo-limbo, Simpson stopper, a lone coconut palm, and a few cabbage palms.

Sure enough, a motorboater was at Darwin's Place, with everything but the kitchen sink. His boom box was blasting out the '80s heavy-metal band *Kiss* to the mangrove trees and the birds. Possum Key had seen it all now. Possum Key is within the confines of the Marjory Stoneman Douglas Wilderness, a federal wilderness established in 1978 and comprising much of the paddling area of Everglades National Park. Normally, motor-operated machines are not allowed in a federally designated wilderness. Here, the water column—that is, anywhere there is water within this particular wilderness—is excepted from the "no motors" wilderness regulation. Thus motorboats can ply the wilderness.

What is wilderness anyway? After 18,600 pages of testimony and the consolidation of sixty-five bills, the Wilderness Act of 1964 was passed. The legal definition of wilderness, spelled out in the bill, is as follows: "A wilderness, in contrast with those areas where man and his . . . works dominate the landscape, is hereby recognized as an area where the earth and its community of life are untrammeled by man, where man . . . is a visitor and does not remain." Romantic but vague, in the grand tradition of government garble.

Like all bills, it was a compromise. Far from ensuring that lands are forever preserved, the bill has loopholes allowing mining and grazing in wilderness areas. The Everglades water column exception is another loophole. But such flaws are tolerated in passing laws to protect the land. One fear that proved unfounded was that wilderness designations would cut lands off from the very citizens who backed them. Ranging from 9.08 million acres to just six acres in size, wilderness areas have multiple uses, such as hiking, hunting, canoeing, climbing, fishing, and camping. Logging, road building, and damming are strictly prohibited. The Marjory Stoneman Douglas Wilderness of Everglades National Park is easily the largest roadless tract in Florida.

The hot afternoon bore down by the time I paddled through the still air of Alligator Creek. Poisonwood trees grew along the banks, adding a tropical touch to the waterway. Also known as the Florida poison tree, it is in the same family as poison ivy. The reddish brown bark is often stained dark by dried sap. The shiny green leaves have characteristic blackish spots on them. Go at a poisonwood tree with a chain saw and you will end up one miserable human being.

Again, I pushed into the winds, traversing Alligator Bay and Dads Bay, into Plate Creek. Gregorio Lopez supposedly named this creek, after dropping a plate here while passing through. Palm-ringed Plate Creek Bay lay ahead. In the bay, backed against a small mangrove island, is the Plate Creek backcountry campsite, built on the pilings of an old land development office dating from the failed land boom of the 1920s. The larger pilings of the shaded portion of the platform are from the old water tower that served the various floating buildings here.

Lostmans Five backcountry campsite lay ahead, my destination. It is a low, sometimes wet piece of ground. It too played a part in land development history. The Tropical Development Company set up shop on nearby Onion Key as headquarters for its new development, known as Poinciana. It was to be the next Miami. Potential land buyers traveled by car to the west side of the Dade County line, where the Tamiami Trail ended, following what is now Loop Road in the Big Cypress National Preserve to the hamlet of Pinecrest. From here, they walked six miles to a canoe landing on the upper reaches of Lostmans Creek, somewhere near the current Lostmans Five campsite. The prospective real estate purchasers were then boated to Onion Key and the office headquarters. This spot is very likely where the development's canoe landing was. The 1926 Hurricane ended the Poinciana development. Lostmans Five was later a site for a fishing cabin atop pilings.

I took a swim in the shallow, mud-bottomed water of Lostmans Five Bay. I was drying off on the dock when a canoe pulled around the bend. To my surprise, the canoe had an outrigger, the first boat of this type I had seen in all my Everglades trips. A bedraggled muddy couple pulled up to the camp and began unloading. Chuck and Cassie had enough stuff to make a motorboater proud. They did have a tiny, ancient motor on the back, but it had quit on their second day out. They were now at day seven. In addition to a motor and paddles they had a third mode of power—a sail. A collapsible mast lay somewhere in the bottom of the boat.

Cassie hailed from Reno, Nevada, and Chuck from Venice, Florida. They were having a good time on their first Everglades trip, though it had been full of unexpected occurrences. First, Cassie had fallen into the mud while loading the boat. Then they had become stuck at low tide not a mile from Flamingo and had had to spend the night in the bottom of the boat beside a mangrove thicket. The next day their boat had swamped while coming around East Cape, nine miles from their starting point. After that

Lostmans Five backcountry campsite lay ahead, my destination.

it had been smooth sailing, going twenty-six miles in one day along Cape Sable to Graveyard Creek. Unfortunately they arrived at midnight, on a low tide, and had to haul their gear through more mud. That was why their clothes and belongings were all plastered with the signature gray Everglades muck.

We exchanged tales as they made their supper. Cassie got the camp stove ready. The stove supposedly used any gas, and they had gas in excess, due to their motor not running. Cassie poured the gas into the stove and Chuck moved forward and put his lighter to it. The ignition flared up into the night sky, then died down. Just as Chuck turned to grab a pot, the stove burst into flames! This was an explosive situation. Chuck dashed to the boat and pulled out a fire extinguisher. I could see the stunned look on his face illuminated by the light of the fire. He aimed the extinguisher then sent the white retardant onto the flaming stove. The fire went out. Good thing they had all that gear. All three of us started talking at once—then the stove caught again! Chuck wheeled around and sprayed the stove once more, this time for twice as long. The stove went out for good. I offered my stove for them to use, but they decided to have a cold supper that evening.

I was heading south again the next morning, still on the Wilderness Waterway. Two Island Bay now had no islands—they had been obliterated by a hurricane. Onion Key lay just ahead. This one-acre island stood in the middle of a small creek connecting Two Island Bay to Onion Key Bay. The high, dry one-acre islet had seen more than a thousand years of human habitation. The Calusa had made a home here, as did a fellow who farmed onions, giving the island its name but moving on to find a more isolated spot. He wasn't around to see the Poinciana development cover the island with wooden buildings that were splintered in the 1926 Hurricane. The island seemed inconspicuous, heavily wooded with Brazilian pepper, buttonwood, and a few palms.

Beyond Onion Key lay another series of bays, running northwest to southeast. I had taken a little too long to get going that morning and was paying the price, as the afternoon winds had kicked up. I dodged among the bay islands, trying to minimize the headwind, and bounced across Rodgers River Bay to make the Rodgers River chickee, temporarily leaving the Wilderness Waterway.

These chickees, backcountry campsites for overnighters at Everglades National Park, are modeled after the chickees that Glades Indians used in time past. In order to adapt to the warm, wet, and buggy conditions, prepark dwellers built thatch-roofed shelters open on four sides, allowing breezes in to cool the chickee and minimize the bugs. Sleeping platforms were elevated, also to keep cool. Skins were used to close the huts in cold weather. The original chickees were built on land. Modern Everglades chickees are built on pilings directly over water, where there is no land for a campsite. They are also open on four sides and have a sloped tin roof. A small gangway leads to an outhouse. Single chickees have one platform and are designed for one party. Double chickees have two platforms and are designed for two parties.

Rodgers River chickee, a bit off the Wilderness Waterway, was a double chickee. The low tide and banging waves made getting out of the kayak and onto the chickee a challenge. I hung onto to the side of the structure and hollered over for assistance from the other fellow already there. He came over and tied up the front of the Old Town. With the sea kayak stabilized, I was able to climb onto the chickee. I thanked Walt and then lay face down on the edge of the chickee, retrieving my gear from the kayak hatches, carefully laying it all out, as the building wind was threatening to push anything and everything into the water.

Walt had retired from NASA and spent his time boating, diving, and generally enjoying Florida's vast water resources. We spent a relaxing evening, telling our life stories, as people sometimes do when out tossed together in the boonies. Such encounters are among the greatest fringe benefits of the outdoor life, chance meetings with interesting people you would ordinarily never encounter.

Overnight, a sea fog obliterated Rogers River Bay. The chickee became a world unto itself. Not even the nearby mangrove shoreline was visible. Walt paddled his canoe north, for Everglades City. I paddled the opposite way, trusting the compass and nautical charts to make Rodgers River. The tides were pushing against me, but I entered the river anyway. The fog slowly dissipated, revealing some stretches of river, blocking out others. The sky cleared as I reached the Cutoff, a narrow waterway connecting Rodgers River to Broad River. The tide was running into the Cutoff. I had a plan—take the Cutoff to the Broad River. Upon arriving at Broad River, I hoped I would find the tide outgoing toward the Gulf, which I hoped to reach. Pelicans squawked as I paddled the Cutoff, interrupting their morning routine. The Broad River lived up to its name here and flowed upstream more strongly than the Rodgers River. My plan wasn't working, so I pulled the kayak astride a sun-bleached log at the river's edge and waited in the shade, taking a little lunch, once again tracing the Wilderness Waterway, waiting for the tide to turn.

A front was coming in, and the wind had shifted to the west. Broad River runs east-west, so the wind was in my face again. The tide waned during my break, and I took off, spotting a few mana-tees plying the river. Ahead was the Broad River backcountry campsite. It had a dock, where I took another break. I was sitting on the dock when a motorboater slowly passed. I hailed him over, asking, "How's the water?"

He knew what water I was talking about. "The Gulf is bad out there. I'm heading inland to fish," he said. His words were on my mind as I left the campsite dock, and I spontaneously turned off the Broad River, away from the Gulf, into what is known as the Nightmare. The Nightmare is a narrow, circuitous route linking the southern and northern Everglades. It is the only water route besides the Gulf connecting Everglades City to Flamingo. The eight-mile route is supposed to be run only on a high tide. The tide was falling rapidly now and was lower in here than I expected. Egrets were perched here and there above the small intercon-nected mud-stained creeks, which oozed with the smell of salt water and decay. The sheltered, shady waterways blocked the winds. I paddled hard, ducking under branches and making quick decisions as to which way to go, trying to beat the ever-shallowing water. Ahead, fallen logs blocked the route. In high water a boat could easily skim over the logs. I had to take the low road, pulling under the logs, scraping myself and the boat with salt muck. I pressed on, not bothering to clean off the muck, then turned down a small creek leading to the Gulf. Better to challenge the winds than getting stuck here in this mosquito haven. It would be hours before the tide rose enough to resume paddling. The considerable likelihood of getting stuck and lost back here is what gave the Nightmare its name.

The muddy tidal creek soon opened to the windy, wavy Gulf, a study in contrast to the Nightmare. I stopped on a shell bank at the Gulf's edge, drinking a little water and getting the mud off my face and clothes. The water had a clear green tint out here and splashed over the boat. The southerly course took me past the Harney River, which connects the salty Gulf to the freshwater Glades on its east-west course. The river was named for Colonel William Harney, who used it for passage to the Gulf in 1840, after crossing the Everglades westward from the Miami River. The Seminoles didn't think the white man could cross the Glades this way, but Harney successfully pursued and slew the tribal leader Chekika, who had conducted his own deadly raid on some white residents at Indian Key during the Seminole Wars.

Southward, the broken mangrove and sand shore stretched out to Shark Point—another great name, short and simple. Waves were banging around the tip of land but did the boat no harm. Just around the corner lay the Graveyard Creek campsite, which overlooks Ponce de Leon Bay. The outgoing tide threatened to cut off Graveyard Creek from Gulf access. At low tide the mouth of Graveyard Creek is a mud flat. Already parts of its floor were exposed. I pressed on toward the mouth of the brown creek, skimming the mud bottom, and made it unaided out of the Gulf and into the deeper waters of Graveyard Creek, where there was a deeper landing out of the wind, backed against a sandy beach. Big tents and heavy gear covered the campsite, indicating motorboat campers. Judging from the numerous beer cans piled in plastic bags hanging from a tree limb, they were having a good time.

I landed the boat and walked into a storm of no-see-ums. The bugs were immediately down my neck and on my legs, hands, and face—on every bit of exposed skin. I tore into the kayak hatch and retrieved the clothes bag, enduring the assault while changing out of my wet, salty paddling clothes into long pants and other clothing that covered my entire body. My outfit included a head net, but I soon found out that its weave was not tight enough. It allowed no-see-ums in. After smearing on bug dope, I walked to the main camping area and found a site facing the Gulf that caught the breeze, minimizing the bugs. Just then the motorboaters roared into camp. The eight men in three boats had been fishing and boozing all day. They were from the East Coast of Florida; only a single Florida native in the bunch. It was their final night in the Glades, and they were going out in style. The setting sun put on a show of its own, coloring the horizon a deep orange before descending below the sea. I listened to their fishing stories, then retired back to my camp and ate supper in the dark, after the no-see-ums had moderated. It was a military meal, an MRE, or meal ready to eat, that Walt had given me back at the Rodgers River chickee. I enjoyed it—but am not known as a picky eater. Quite the opposite, as friends and family will attest.

Luckily for me, I had an incoming tide the next morning, which allowed quick Gulf access. Otherwise paddlers have to stroke up Graveyard Creek in a circuitous route to reach Ponce De Leon Bay, emerging near the mouth of Shark River, rather than taking the Gulf. Strong north winds were predicted, necessitating an early start. Ponce de Leon Bay stretched three miles across and was deep enough to cause a paddler trouble. I bid farewell to the motorboaters and hit the bay, power paddling across the expanse of water, mostly beating the wind. Waves were piling up near Shark River Island but subsided once the boat passed onto the western shore of the Gulf Coast. Cape Sable lay to the south. I soon reached its most northerly point, Northwest Cape, and stopped at the beach lying between the turquoise Gulf waters and the tawny prairie dotted with palm trees and other small tree islands. Northwest Cape displayed a *real* beach, a natural coastline, so rare in these times. Seagrass, shells, and driftwood scattered over the tan sand of crushed shell, not some antiseptic pumped-in white stuff that looks pretty ten stories down.

Northwest Cape curved outward to a small point, then arced inward again. It was here that I ate lunch, on a fine Everglades day. Thin clouds spread over the land and sea. The tide lines of sea fodder made narrow bands along the beach. A flock of terns gathered on the beach, waiting for me to eat before they resumed their lunch of small fish. Back in the boat, I curved along with the coastline, staying in close to the waves, which were patiently taking turns meeting with the edge of the continent. On land, a gopher tortoise lumbered toward some unseen destination. This species is one of only four tortoises of the United States to occur east of the Mississippi River. The gopher tortoise ranges from southern Florida to lower Georgia and west to southern Mississippi and a small portion of Louisiana.

This ancient animal prefers well-drained sandy soils and dry habitats like pine flatwoods, sand pine scrub woods, and coastal dune areas. These are also the habitats suitable for development in Florida, which creates pressure on the gopher tortoise. Florida now has only one-third of the gopher tortoise population of days gone by. This slow-moving creature is best known for digging an impressive burrow, which can be forty feet long and ten feet deep. The burrow provides a haven from heat and cold and the periodic wildfires that sweep through tortoise territory. Eventually snakes, mice, rabbits, and many other animals inhabit tortoise burrows. The burrow has become an important habitat component for a community of animals besides the gopher tortoise itself.

From birth, it takes a tortoise nearly as long as a person to mature. The odds of an egg reaching maturity are slim. After mating, adult female tortoises lay from three to fifteen eggs. Many are eaten by raccoons and other animals. The young that do hatch will live in or near their mother's burrow, but many are eaten at this stage. Tortoise hatchlings that survive coyotes, raccoons, and humans can live more than forty years. Loss of habitat is threatening the animal's existence, as are automobiles, monoculture forestry, and being eaten by people. And since the gopher tortoise burrow is an important element for many other life forms in its habitat, if the tortoise is gone and can't build its burrow, then what happens to all the rest? Luckily for this particular gopher tortoise, its home was a national park and it did not face the same threats as its brethren elsewhere.

On the shore near the tortoise were sparsely leaved gumbo-limbo trees. Their wind-sculpted branches rose above the beach-side brush, growing where sand and soil intertwined. In lower spots, behind the beach, mangrove took its appointed place, where the land was sometimes land but sometimes marsh, never allowing itself to be just land or water. This is just where mangrove grew.

Farther down, Middle Cape came to a sharp point cut by deeper waters. Campers in motorboats like Middle Cape, since their craft stand much less chance of being left high and dry during tidal extremes. Here, families were rambling around on the beach, perched in chairs beside tents, and reading beneath sun shelters. An American flag planted on the beach waved in the breeze, proclaiming this one of the finest pieces of real estate in North America.

Sporadic yet certain hurricanes had renewed the cape's natural appearance and covered signs of human impact on the land. The name Palm Point preceded its current name of Middle Cape. Before nautical charts, loran, and global positioning systems, the palms of Palm Point were a navigational point of certainty until they were cut down by vandals in the early 1800s. An old well, dug perhaps by the Calusa or by pirates, stood behind the point. Fresh water floated over the salt water just a few feet down and too much pumping would yield brackish water. This well also served the men at Middle Cape's Fort Cross, a small garrison erected in the

1850s as part of the Seminole War effort. There were agricultural and homesteading efforts here too. James Waddell of Key West began a coconut plantation in the 1880s. He planted thousands of trees, which became the marker for the cape for decades afterward. Upon the trees' maturing, some coconut shipments were made to Miami and Tampa, but the plantation and its outbuildings passed from one caretaker to the next until the 1935 Hurricane blew the trees away. Vegetable farmers living in palmetto-thatched shacks planted the lands for the Key West market but their operations were small and not ongoing. A brief exception occurred during the Civil War when the Union, which held Key West, sent men to grow food on the cape for the Key West troops. The Raulerson brothers tried cattle grazing on the marl (read: salty mud) flat off the beach, giving the place the name Raulerson Prairie. Mosquitoes tormented the cattle, and the lack of nutritious grass caused this operation to fail also. Storms and hurricanes that lashed the cape swept salt water over the land, sterilizing the soil until rains leached out the salt. Cape Sable is as unforgiving as it is beautiful.

The following wind inspired my desire to continue paddling, and soon I made my way past the old dock at East Cape. This dock was a leftover from a tour boat that ran out of Flamingo in the early days of the national park. Fort Poinsett, also part of the Seminole War effort, once stood here, until all remains of it were blown away in the 1935 Hurricane.

The Miami land boom of the early 1920s reached Cape Sable. Ideas were hatched to drain the cape for more homesite potential. The state of Florida promised land to the East Coast Railroad Company in exchange for constructing the railroad along the Atlantic Ocean. Model Land Company, which handled property for East Coast, began planning development of the cape. They built a road from Florida City toward the cape. The Homestead Canal ran along this road and reached west into the lakes behind the cape. Other drainage canals were dug into Florida Bay. The Mid Cape and East Cape canals were dug to drain Cape Sable. But the canals never worked properly, draining during the wet season but allowing saltwater intrusion during dry times. In some places the canals widened, and are still widening to this day, especially Mid Cape and East Cape canals, which have altered the ratio of salt to fresh water in Lake Ingraham and other waters behind Cape Sable.

East Cape marks the southwesternmost point of the Florida mainland. The coast turns here from north-south to east-west. The wind turned into my bow, and I didn't care. Where else would I rather be? The paddling wore on me as I had reached the twenty-mile mark, but not too far ahead lay Clubhouse Beach, my destination. First came East Cape Canal and House Ditch. If the 1926 Hurricane hadn't collapsed the land boom, high-rises might have been here, too.

Mostly mangrove shoreline rimmed the land beyond East Cape. Clubhouse Beach was out there somewhere. This beach was so named for the Model Land Company's practice of boating people to the edge of Florida Bay and taking them to a clubhouse where they were served meals. The prospects were then driven over the marl prairie by car to see the land. This locale, like the rest of the Cape Sable area, was condemned for park land in the 1940s.

This beach wasn't near the glory of Cape Sable's sandy swaths. Few beaches are, though. Clubhouse displayed just a sliver of sand, sandwiched by a wooded coast. The sand divided the shallow water of Florida Bay and a prairie of low-lying, bright green pickleweed framed in buttonwood and more mangrove. I pulled the boat ashore and was greeted by a backpacker who had hiked the Coastal Prairie Trail to Clubhouse Beach from Flamingo.

Jim Baker was his name. His white hair and white beard gave him a distinctive look. Jim was an environmental lobbyist from Washington state. We compared outdoor notes. I noticed the sky darkening, turning gray, then black. Rain was coming. Tents went

I noticed the sky darkening, turning gray, then black. Rain was coming.

up with haste and soon I entered my plastic refuge, trying to fight sleep. I wanted to leave slumbering for the night. Just before dusk, the drops ceased and I made dinner, the usual noodle concoction. After the front had pushed through, revealing a freshly washed mural of stars, Jim came out for a visit. I sat on the kayak eating the slop as he pointed up to a moving speck.

"See that? It's a satellite. Over there, that's Venus. And the two bright steady lights, one on top of the other, are Jupiter and Saturn. It's a rich time for viewing planets." He showed me constellations and explained that for reasons unknown to himself or his parents, he had decided that what was up there in the sky was important. He needed to know about it. So he got a telescope and had been enamored ever since.

Jim was still in his tent as I paddled away from Clubhouse Beach in the morning, thinking about our conversation. So much to learn, so little time. The coast jutted outward and I passed over a place called the Sawfish Hole. A group of blacks lived near here during the early twentieth century, cutting wood and making charcoal. A sailor from nearby Flamingo shipped the charcoal to Key West. The plentiful sawfish of the area tore up nets used to catch sea turtles, ruining the nets with their teeth-laden snouts. Have you ever seen a sawfish? In shape it looks like a cross between a shark and a ray, flat, but with fins and a tail. From this odd body protrudes a snout containing twenty-four or more pairs of teeth. The sawfish uses them to slash side to side through schools of fish. It then comes back and consumes the injured. If you ever find a sawfish on the end of your fishing line, cut the line. They can do some damage if mishandled.

Winds turn clockwise in our hemisphere. This means the wind can never go from west to south to east to north, only from west to north to east to south. They go counterclockwise in the southern hemisphere. The wind had shifted to the east and picked up. The shallows were rife with sharks, their dorsal fins and tail fins sometimes breaking the wave-riddled surface. I paddled forward and bumped into one of the ancient swimmers, both of us receiving a startling jolt of adrenaline.

I had to get far from shore to get a paddle into the water. Even then the lack of depth prevented a good solid stroke. The normally clear Florida Bay had become chocolate milk. The seven miles passed slowly. When Flamingo Campground finally came into view, there was a problem: the vast expanse of seagrass, shells, and mud, known as the sea floor, lying between the campground and me. The outgoing tide and east wind had simply blown the water from Florida Bay. The time came to get down and dirty. I hopped out of the boat, aimed it toward dry land, and began slopping across the flat. At each footstep I sank into gray-brown sludge above knee level. Sometimes I pushed the boat from behind; sometimes I pulled from the front with a rope. The best method of mud travel was to put my weight on the kayak and push forward. This wasn't the best thing for the floor of Florida Bay, but I was determined to land at this campground as it was my overnight destination. My only other option was to paddle the channel into Flamingo marina, which was a mile or more from the campground. And I wasn't keen on leaving the boat there. Instead, I determinedly moved toward the line of tents and RVs. As I neared land, the campground kiosk came into view. Beside it stood a familiar figure. After bringing the boat to shore, covered in mud, I hollered out, "John!"

John Haapala is a Minnesotan and had been a long-time volunteer in the Flamingo Campground. He and his wife Barb and I had become friends while I was working on the Everglades paddling guide. I was a fair distance off and wearing a big sun hat. John didn't know who I was me at first, but soon enough he recognized my Tennessee accent. Barb came out of the kiosk and gave me a hug. The familiar and friendly faces were a great sight. They invited me to camp with them and I happily took up the offer, after scrubbing off the mud.

The day passed fast, visiting with this couple from Hibbing, way up north in Bob Dylan country. Barb and John had raised a family. They had their Nordic sensibilities and reservations but also wanted to enjoy life. They wintered in the park, then headed back north, where John would refill the bank account as an iron worker.

I pedaled around on John's bike, meeting up with some park employees who were friends, too, Roy Wood and Steve Robinson among them. I planned to stick around Flamingo for a few days, being a campground "regular" who put in an annual appearance.

While I was visiting the backcountry office, a paddler getting a backcountry permit was waving my book around. John Waters, another friend and park ranger, pointed me out as the author of the book. I signed the book for Cassandra and helped her plot out a route. She was going into town for supplies, which also I needed, and I asked her for a ride; she happily obliged. But the traffic and rush, rush, rush South Florida scene shocked me. It was none too soon that we were pulling into Flamingo again. I was very ready to head out on the last leg of the trip, bound for the Keys.

That evening Barb, John, and I went to the tenters' part of the Flamingo Campground to visit Chuck Dees, of Illinois, an Everglades regular who had been coming down here annually for more than a quarter century. Chuck was shark fishing. The tides were perfect for it tonight. He had just set up as we arrived. Lanterns glowed brightly from the picnic table, illuminating Chuck as he baited a big old hook with mullet. Then he put his rod in the industrial-strength holder, hopped into a little skiff, and rowed the bait into the dark bay. He dropped the mullet into an old hole in the bay where former Flamingo residents had dynamited the bottom to deepen the waters for their boats. Chuck then rowed back and sat with the rest of us. It wasn't long before the reel began to click, followed by click-click-click, then a full-blown run of line whizzing off the reel. Chuck bounced up and grabbed the rod, setting the hook with a fierce pull. The fight began. Chuck retreated from the water, gaining a bit of slack, then reeled in line as he walked back toward the edge. Backwards he went, rod bending. Sweat poured from his forehead. He threw off his cap and continued the battle. The shark was losing and was coming ever closer to the shoreline. Chuck left the grassy shore and descended to the mud. There the battle ended. After making sure all the fight was out of the shark, he hauled it to the picnic table, where it stretched beyond both ends of the boards.

"Lemon shark," declared John as he and Chuck set about gutting, skinning, and cleaning it. They planned to have a cookout the following night.

A cool breeze swept through the campground late that evening. Nights like this were welcome for campers and even more so for full-time residents of Flamingo in prepark days. There is no evidence of Calusa having had major settlements on this low marl prairie overlooking Florida Bay. Though rich in marine food sources, the Flamingo area was too open to deadly winds and accompanying flooding, although a few outlying keys protect Flamingo somewhat. Whites settled here anyway in the late 1800s. They even got a post office in 1893. The settlers sought bounty from sea and land, fishing the bay, growing sugarcane, and cutting the buttonwood trees for charcoal. They would harvest the buttonwood, pile it up, and light it, then cover it up with dirt, allowing it to smolder and become charcoal. They shipped the charcoal to Key West to be sold for cooking and heating fuel.

Life at this most southerly community on the United States mainland challenged its residents. Mosquitoes were a constant problem, especially in the rainy season. The heat bore down incessantly. There were no stores. All communications and supplies were via boat. A road made it down here in 1922, but it was so muddy as to be useless in the rainy season. Fish and produce continued to be taken to market by boat until the 1940s, when fish trucks began taking the haul to market by road, adding another contact with the outside world. But the days of old Flamingo were numbered with the establishment of Everglades National Park in 1947.

Making Everglades National Park a reality took immense effort. Economic forces were already building, from fishermen in Flamingo, loggers in the Pinelands, clammers in the Ten Thousand Islands, plume hunters in Cuthbert Rookery, real estate developers plotting lots on Cape Sable, and farmers growing vegetables on the on the fringes. Most South Floridians were generally for a park, except where it got in the way of their making money. But the tourism potential for South Florida of an Everglades park worked in the favor of establishing such a preserve.

Actual preservation in the Everglades region came as early as 1916. The royal palms and superlatively attractive vegetation of an island within the sawgrass east of Homestead had gained the attention of the Florida Federation of Women's Clubs. Known then as Paradise Key, the island became Royal Palm State Park. This marked the first time land had actually been set aside in the Everglades. In 1905, the Audubon Society had placed rangers near Flamingo to protect bird rookeries, but the land itself hadn't been under protection.

The idea of a national park in Florida gained steam. The Koreshans had editorialized for such a park, as had the newly formed Florida Society of Natural History. Enter Earnest Coe, who had moved to Miami and now became acquainted with the members of the natural history society. He then formed another organization, the Tropical Everglades National Park Association. Just a year later, in 1929, the Florida Legislature backed the formation of a commission to study the establishment of a national park. It sounds like nothing much more than a bunch of people meeting and talking and not much happening, but the word was spreading. Later in 1929, the U.S. Congress formed another committee to study the possibility of a national park somewhere in South Florida. National park personnel came down to the Everglades in 1930, exploring by air, land, and water, and submitting a report to Congress. The Great Depression slowed things down again, but a bill establishing an Everglades park was signed into law by FDR in mid-1934. The catch: no money would be appropriated to purchase land for the park for at least five years. Many officials thought it silly to waste money on park land during such hard times. The boundaries that Congress approved then were much larger than the park of today, encompassing all of Key Largo, much of the reef of the Keys, and a good piece north of the Tamiami Trail, site of present-day Big Cypress National Preserve.

Earnest Coe spoke in front of any group who would listen, promoting the idea of a park in the Everglades, pressing on for these larger pieces of land. He saw the unique nature of Florida's reefs and wanted them protected, too. But his insistence on the larger park created enemies and caused a backlash against the park proposal. The country focused on World War II, again halting the park effort. Land cost much more after the war than beforehand, for a land boom hit after so many GIs had seen the lure of the Sunshine State's landscape while training for the war. It ended up costing more to get the current 1.5 million acres of park than it would have cost for more than 2 million acres under consideration had the land been bought before the war.

Florida's governor Millard Caldwell agreed to turn over state land in the Everglades to the federal government. The postwar U.S. Congress appointed and funded a managing director, and the state legislature provided funds to purchase private holdings within the park. On December 6, 1947, Harry Truman came down to what is now Everglades City and dedicated the Everglades National Park. Land acquisition continues today, and together the state of Florida and the federal government have begun a thirty-year plan to restore the Everglades ecosystem and its waterways to conditions more closely resembling those when the Calusa were roaming the River of Grass.

I wasn't going to enjoy the steaks from Chuck's lemon shark. It was time to head south. The following morning I left modern Flamingo with its electricity, tap water, marina, parking lots, and lodge and paddled into the heart of Florida Bay, realizing that had the park not been established, Flamingo would be a lot bigger than it is already. John, Barb, and Chuck were going fishing, this time by boat. They accompanied me on my paddle out of Flamingo. We bid farewell near Murray Key. Another good-bye. On I went into the open Florida Bay. The water was exceedingly shallow for being so open, but a rising tide and the absence of wind held promise for a paddler.

I entered the Murray-Clive Channel, a natural channel running between deeper sections of Florida Bay. Many places in Florida Bay, such as near Flamingo Campground, go dry at low tide. The term *bank* is used for these large flats. I followed the channel south and reached Clive Key, at the western edge of Dildo Key Bank, one of the aforementioned tidal flats. The sun's burners were already on high as I ate lunch in the shade of a mangrove on the island's edge. The water deepened in a basin south of Clive Key. Fish abruptly scattered and seagrass waved as I paddled on, passing Johnson Key to my left. With the rising tide, more water than land spread over the horizon.

Rabbit Key Basin, a wide deep area, lay just past Man of War Key. I had it made from here. Overhead, a flock of roseate spoonbills passed. These pink birds are often mistaken for flamingos, especially around Flamingo. They use their flattened bills to swing side to side in shallows searching for fish, insects, larvae, and small crustaceans. Flamingos do nest in the Bahamas and West Indies but are rare in Florida. A flamingo has a much longer neck than a spoonbill, long legs, and a curved beak.

The Old Town cut a wake through the planed, mostly still waters. Ahead the clearing and dock of Little Rabbit Key were visible. The midafternoon sun blared onto the splintery planks. The warmth bled through to my feet as I debarked, pulled my shirt off. I jumped into the water. Relief! I drippingly unloaded the boat, pulled it onto land, and dove headfirst into the bay, swimming beneath the sea, making like a porpoise for the open water. I popped out of the water and was a good distance from the dock. The tide pushed fast and strong, threatening to take me away. I kicked and

On I went into the open Florida Bay.

stroked with force as the water pushed around the north side of the island. I stopped my backward flow and made headway, eventually returning to the dock with a new respect for the tides in Florida Bay.

Land exploration might be a little safer, I decided. I followed a path beneath the mangrove that ringed the island save for the cleared area by the dock. Schools of snapper hugged the edge of Little Rabbit Key, waiting for the flowing tide to deliver dinner. A miniature marl prairie occupied the center of the island. After exploring I sat on the dock and looked out on the bay. Water had been my constant companion since the Okefenokee Swamp in Georgia, down the Suwannee to the Gulf and down the Gulf to the Keys. Tomorrow I would reach a new body of water—the Atlantic Ocean.

I saw a speck on the horizon. A boat was in the distance, coming my way. The glint of a paddle reflected in the late evening light.

After exploring I sat on the dock and looked out on the bay. Water had been my constant companion since the Okefenokee Swamp in Georgia, down the Suwannee to the Gulf and down the Gulf to the Keys.

Another paddler at Little Rabbit Key? Up to the dock arrived a man in his forties. With nary another person for miles, I had to engage him in conversation. A casual "Whatcha doin' out here?" was my opener.

The man got up from his boat with a slight grimace. "Been down paddling the Glades for a week," he said, stretching. "A big national park . . . it almost rates up there with my favorite one back home in California." If this was his way to lure me into asking more questions, it worked. A map in his hand and boat full of camping gear revealed that we shared a passion.

Tim was a tall, lithe man with dark skin and a shock of brown hair that resembled a Brillo pad. His desert compadres called him Seldom Seen Tim, for his propensity to head to the most isolated lands in the West. The nickname may have been a rip-off from an old Edward Abbey book, but it probably stuck the first time anyone called him that.

"Where in California?" I asked, unable to control my curiosity.

"Death Valley National Park is my main haunt, but deserts all over are my game," he said. "I did the Boy Scout and Explorer thing, where us hardcores eventually formed a climbing club. I went to MIT and got an engineering degree in between playing tiddlywinks."

I laughed at that.

"No really, our team won three national championships and one year beat the bloody British for the world crown. Then I returned to Fresno and started my own business designing computer software."

How did a tiddlywinks-playing desert-rat engineer end up in the Everglades? He had read Edward Abbey's *A Walk in the Desert Hills,* about an extended hike in Arizona. It was not an especially exciting trip but a long and lonely one. "It appealed to me," said Tim. "Fifteen years ago I took off for six days into the Death Valley backcountry, the 'other' Death Valley. I survived and was hooked. Suddenly there was a mass of things to do in the desert." Most people avoided that experience, he told me, passing through the desert only to reach the neon Mecca of artificiality, Las Vegas, seeing the desert as a boring wasteland to be endured until they entered a casino muttering, "Oh, mama, I feel lucky tonight!"

He enjoyed the freedom of roaming the ostensibly less desirable places. The Everglades were once thought of as a place good only for drainage. Where was the biggest roadless area? Where were the fewest people? "I like to go to the blankest spots on the map," Tim summed up. He had raised his tone; his eyes had become even more alive. A blue vein bulged from his neck. Taut muscles in his arms moved beneath his skin. His hands played about while he talked.

The desert of Death Valley is vast, yet the canyons can be quite intimate, he went on. Most people consider the place ugly and hostile, but with familiarity comes beauty and peace. The land is open and bare with long vistas, but up close there are curious and fascinating formations, hidden corners. And water in a land where it is so rare makes it even more precious and charming. In the Everglades, it is land that is precious, he observed.

Back in the Tennessee hills, I told him, abundant water grows a different landscape—green forests and white, frothy waterfalls. Autumn's colorful trees, secretive salamanders, black bears digging for squaw root, trout at the bottom of a crystalline pool, mossy-backed logs decaying in the shade.

Tim pointed outward, "The Everglades are beautiful to me. To others, the Everglades are a hostile, forbidding place. This place is a prime example of beauty coming with familiarity."

We shared the campsite picnic table, cooking dinner under lantern light. Tim retired to his tent while I sat on the edge of the dock overlooking Florida Bay. The bug invasion never happened, though mosquitoes had drained me on a previous trip to this backcountry campsite. Fireflies by the hundreds blinked in the clearing. The red flashing beacon of Flamingo blinked across the bay thirteen miles away. The glow of Miami was probably fifty miles distant. The Keys were a lighted string to the east and south. The Keys. They had seemed so immensely distant as I contemplated paddling there from up north. It was hard to believe, but I would be there tomorrow.

The conversation with Tim had me thinking again about why this trip. It's like trying to explain why you love someone. It can't really be described succinctly—only with broad strokes. Scenes and feelings stay with me and draw me back for more: a new riverside camp with a strange outline of black clouds against an infinite sky; a cup of coffee next to a friendly fire; a moonlit landscape. Such images mixed with elements of adventure are the recipe of a wilderness experience, unattainable online, on TV, or any damn place except the real thing. In this case, the layers of civilization were checked at the edge of the water. As the civilized veneer is stripped away, your needs become simplified. It's the original real world. The earth functioned fine before being tracked with roads, ripped with plows, dug up, leveled, and fenced in. Society, obligations, bills, clocks, and propriety melt away and are forgotten.

Out here I lived by the sun, transported by muscle, feeling the vastness of the natural world. My milieu. It took me a long time to get here. And how much more I appreciated it. Its beauty surrounded me and embraced me. Out here, I lived at the water's pace, by the water's rules, and ultimately with a water state of mind.

The Everglades are beautiful. Yellowstone is beautiful. So are the Tetons. So are the Smokies. Beyond the beauty are elements of adventure and freedom in the Everglades—a chance to be individualistic, the need to be responsible. Centuries ago when Europeans began to settle Florida, there were no roads. No motels. No accurate maps. No roadside attractions. People died of disease, heat, cold, Indians, and snakes. They were buried and the rest moved on. Now parts of the Everglades have park service visitor centers, air conditioning, cruise control, and nature trails. Someone trips over a rock at a scenic turnout, and their lawyer sues somebody for millions. How far we've come in such a short time. But much of the area still provides classic elements of adventure. Paddling here has inherent risk, the possibility of getting lost, being swamped, dying. That is the kick—the high we can find in Death Valley, Florida Bay, or Grizzly Creek.

The concept of adventure has been watered down in recent years. Remember Stanley, Byrd, Hillary, McKenzie, or Lewis and Clark? Their adventures had challenge, risk, uncertainty, responsibility. Sometimes you find or achieve something great. Sometimes you fail or mess up and are happy to get home in one piece. Now we have scores of "adventure travel" companies: show up with your toothbrush and bathing suit, and they'll provide you with the experience of adventure. Wrong. You've paid your money to eliminate the risk and for someone else to take the responsibility. It's not adventure; it's a ride. There's a difference between an adventure and a vacation. It all depends on how you get there, physically and spiritually.

An adventure starts at home with a place and an idea. You come up with a plan of where to explore, and you put together an outing. You decide what to take, what not to take, who to take, how long to be gone, and the best way to get from point A to point B. The onus is on your own shoulders. All the decisions are yours and your neck is on the line if the plan fails. Uncertainty. Risk. Challenge. Responsibility. Fear and a dry throat. The elements of true adventure.

Warm winds picked up during the night. I hastily loaded and was on the water before the sun breached the horizon. Tim snoozed in his tent. I skirted the narrow channel just north of Little Rabbit Key and paddled southeast along the edge of Ninemile Bank. Ahead was Barnes Key. The kayak rolled and swayed past the wide mangrove land. In the distance, the Long Key Viaduct rose from the water, made an arc, and descended back into the water. The land under the viaduct bridge was not yet visible from the low perspective of the sea kayak. I then turned due south for the Buchanan Keys. Twin Key Bank blocked my path. The paddle could hardly gain purchase in seagrass-tipped water less than a foot deep. Progress slowed further around the Buchanan Keys. They had their own flats. The flats, sandbars, reefs, and rocks here have wrecked many boats plying the Keys.

The first to bear the brunt of these waters in earnest were the Spaniards, as they passed through the Florida Straits en route to Europe, splintering their wooden hulls in the night or being blown into obstacles by the black whirling storms of hurricane season.

The Calusa could mostly avoid these watery hazards with smaller canoes and lifelong local knowledge of the waters. The Calusa swept in after the wrecks. These first salvagers took the treasures of the Central and South American Indians, not knowing their value across the water but trading the booty among themselves and with Indians at points north. They also took surviving Spaniards as hostages, killing some and assimilating others into their way of life.

Salvaging would became an important business all along the Florida Keys, especially Key West. It made sense—all travel in the area was by boat until Henry Flagler extended his East Coast Rail-road to Key West. He connected the port to the mainland via thirty-eight bridges, completing his "Eighth Wonder of the World" on January 22, 1912. Flagler's railroad brought passengers and supplies down to the Keys until 1935, when it was destroyed by the Labor Day Hurricane that blew at two hundred miles per hour, spreading death as well as destroying the railroad.

The blue-bright waters deepened and the waves grew as I made for Channel Five, which runs beneath the Long Key Viaduct. The pilings of Flagler's old railroad stood beside the newer Long Key Viaduct. The railroad had neared Long Key in 1906. Flagler built screened cottages on Long Key for his workers while they labored on the viaduct. Some employees were housed in floating barges near Long Key, called quarterboats. When a hurricane hit in 1906, one of these quarterboats came loose from its moorings and was swept to sea. More than a hundred men were drowned. After the Long Key Viaduct was finished, Flagler turned the construction camp into a fishing camp, establishing the Long Key Fishing Club. He added a lodge along the oceanside beach and a little narrow gauge railroad that cut across the island. The club's most famous visitor was Zane Grey, the western novelist. Grey first arrived in 1913 and began organizing angling tournaments that promoted catch-and-release fishing.

Grey single-handedly popularized sailfish angling. At the time sailfish were an undesirable catch. They were known as "boo-hoos," because of the disappointment when they were caught or for fouling lines intended for other fish. He went after these attractive predators with light tackle, enjoying their acrobatic leaps. The sailfish is now the Florida state saltwater fish.

After the Labor Day Hurricane, the Key West Extension was not rebuilt. However, the railroad pilings were used for a road bridge that subsequently connected Key West to the mainland, ending its era of isolation. Today, U.S. Highway 1 carries traffic day and night, also bearing the water pipeline that brings the islands their precious aqua. The individual low bridge pilings separated as I neared Channel Five and perspective changed. Discerning distant objects is a constant challenge for boaters, as things don't always look the same from afar as from up close. Up close it seemed an easy passage between the pilings of the old bridge and the larger, more widely spaced pilings of the new viaduct. The waves had picked up in the open water and were surprisingly rough near the bridge. A tide ripped between Long Key and Craig Key, pushing me about as I negotiated the bridge. The Old Town shot past the last piling and there it was—the Atlantic Ocean.

I couldn't believe it.

It didn't look too different from Florida Bay, perhaps a little bluer, perhaps a little rougher, but there it was, the Atlantic Ocean. The buoys of crab traps in the channel were straining on their ropes, pushing toward the Atlantic. To my right stood the island of Long Key, where the fishing club and a coconut plantation on the island were destroyed with the railroad in 1935. Here the state of Florida has established the Long Key State Recreation Area, my end point.

Indian Key, a few miles north of here, had played a notable role in Keys history. On Indian Key, Jacob Houseman decided to establish his own wrecking center. The Gulf Stream flowed close to the

Near Long Key Point I landed the Old Town on the beach and got out. To the east rolled the Atlantic Ocean.

reefs here, placing Houseman close to many wrecks. His plan worked, making him wealthy and making his competition at Key West angry, especially when he got the state to form Dade County with Indian Key as the county seat. Can you imagine little old Indian Key as the county seat of Miami-Dade County today? In time, the Key Westers of Monroe County took Houseman to court and finally drove him out of business.

Once past Long Key Bight, I curved south along the Atlantic, hanging close to the shore of Long Key. Near Long Key Point I landed the Old Town on the beach and got out. To the east rolled the Atlantic Ocean. The Atlantic where the Calusa had paddled their long cypress dugout canoes, where Spaniards had been harassed by pirates, where the Union had watched for officials of the Confederate government escaping to Cuba after the Civil War, where Chinese were smuggled into the United States after staging in Havana, where submarines had watched for Germans in World War II, and now the place where I was finishing my journey.

The memories flooded like an August hurricane. In the end all we have are memories. What these shores had seen; what I had seen along the trip. Florida has undergone incredible changes over time, and the changes come ever faster. My brain reeled with ponderables. The relationship between humanity and nature, the modern condition; water, development, preservation; the past, the future . . .

There are times in life when you have experiences that open up a new world you never knew existed. And this new world has to be reworked into your tenets. Or your tenets have to be reworked into the new world. Today, it is primarily people who make changes to the land. Florida is now the country's third most populous state. The swift and sure alteration of the landscape is threatening the real Florida, which undergoes change on nature's schedule, in nature's sense of time. Time perception is a funny thing. It all depends on what you put in between the hours, days, seasons, and years. It adds up to your life. But as sure as the Suwannee flows to the sea, and the waves lap against the peninsula, Florida's history remains.

The following maps show detailed areas of my trip south, represented here by the dotted line.

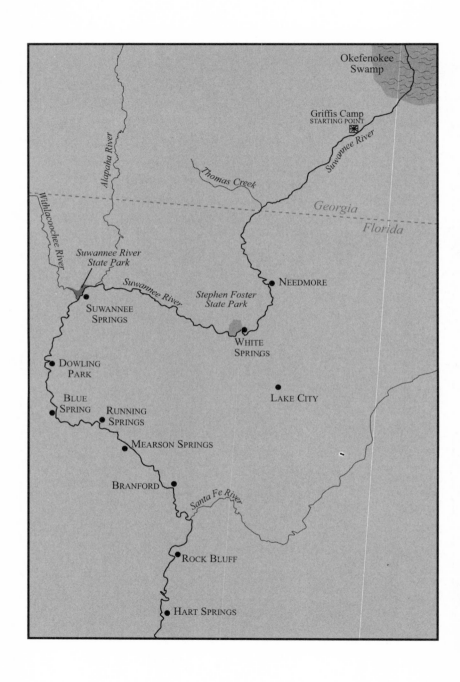

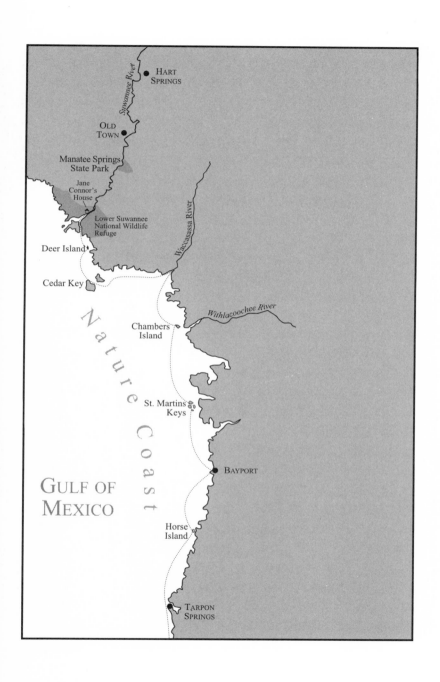

HART
SPRINGS

Suwannee River

OLD
TOWN

Manatee Springs
State Park

Jane
Connor's
House

Waccasassa River

Lower Suwannee
National Wildlife
Refuge

Deer Island

Cedar Key

Chambers
Island

Withlacoochee River

St. Martins
Keys

BAYPORT

Horse
Island

GULF OF
MEXICO

Nature Coast

TARPON
SPRINGS

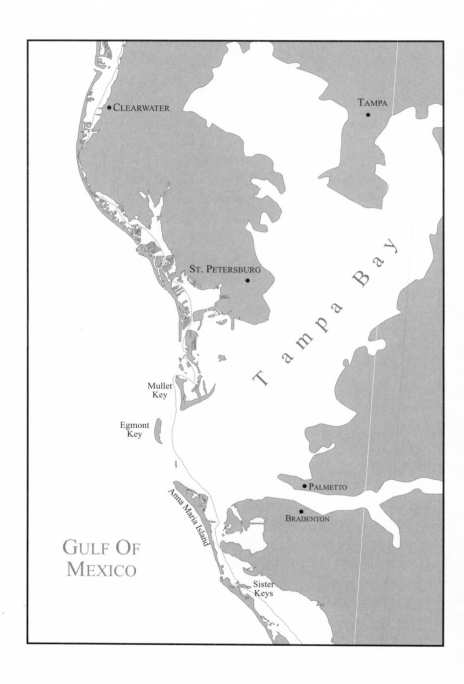

CLEARWATER

TAMPA

ST. PETERSBURG

T a m p a   B a y

Mullet
Key

Egmont
Key

PALMETTO

BRADENTON

GULF OF
MEXICO

Anna Maria Island

Sister
Keys

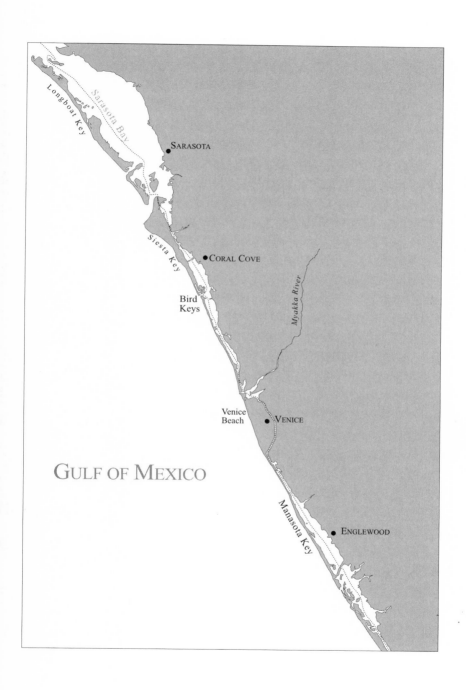

GULF OF MEXICO

Longboat Key

Sarasota Bay

● SARASOTA

Siesta Key

● CORAL COVE

Bird
Keys

Myakka River

Venice
Beach

● VENICE

Manasota Key

● ENGLEWOOD

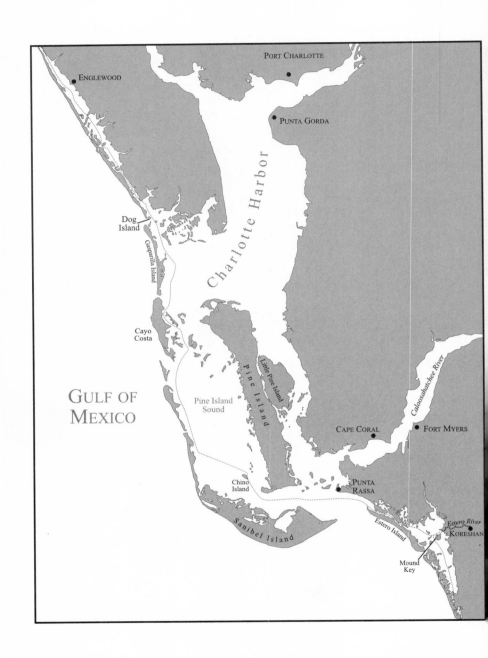

PORT CHARLOTTE

ENGLEWOOD

PUNTA GORDA

Charlotte Harbor

Dog
Island

Gasparilla Island

Cayo
Costa

Caloosahatchee River

Little Pine Island

Pine Island

GULF OF
MEXICO

Pine Island
Sound

CAPE CORAL

FORT MYERS

Chino
Island

PUNTA
RASSA

Sanibel Island

Estero Island

Estero River
KORESHAN

Mound
Key

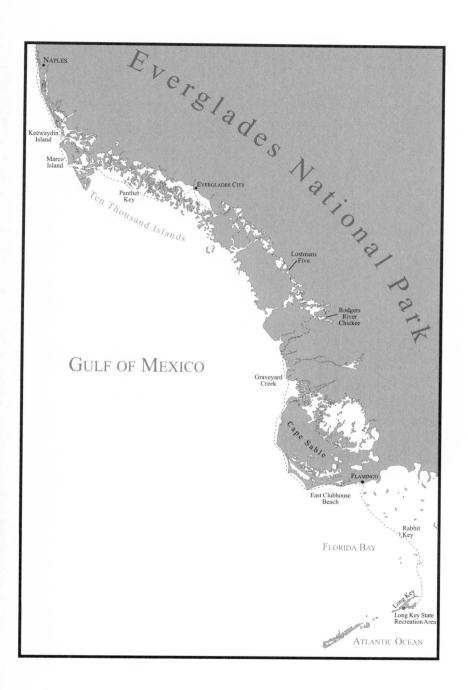

NAPLES

Keewaydin
Island

Marco
Island

Everglades National Park

EVERGLADES CITY

Panther
Key

Ten Thousand Islands

Lostmans
Five

Rodgers
River
Chickee

GULF OF MEXICO

Graveyard
Creek

Cape Sable

FLAMINGO

East Clubhouse
Beach

Rabbit
Key

FLORIDA BAY

Long Key

Long Key State
Recreation Area

ATLANTIC OCEAN

Johnny Molloy is an outdoor writer and adventurer based in Nashville, Tennessee. He has written seventeen outdoor hiking and paddling books, including *Beach and Coastal Camping in Florida* (UPF, 1999), *A Paddler's Guide to Everglades National Park* (UPF, 2000), and *The Hiking Trails of Florida's National Forests, Parks, and Preserves* (UPF, 2001).